Desk Reference Handbook For Christian School Administrators

Desk Reference Handbook For Christian School Administrators

By
Kathryn J. Perry, Ed.D., Ph.D.

Table of Contents

ACKNOWLEDGEMENTS

The writing of this book was made possible with the help and support of Dr. Glenn Mollette and Dr. Keith Wilhite who provided guidance and direction. I also want to give thanks to my daughter, Jennifer, who encouraged me in this pursuit. I especially want to thank my husband, Pastor William Perry, for his encouragement, guidance, patience, suggestions, and continual assistance. Without him this endeavor would not have been possible. Most of all I want to thank my Lord Jesus Christ for calling me into this work and supplying the way of obtaining the necessary resources.

Chapter One:
A Vision For Christian Education

Proverbs 3:5-6 "Trust in the Lord with all your heart and lean not on your own understanding; in all your ways acknowledge him, and he will make your paths straight." [1]

Christian Education, or perhaps better stated, "Christ in Education," is not a new phenomenon. I like the way Walter G. Fremont describes the first classroom, students, and teacher:

"Once there was a perfect classroom with perfect students and a perfect Teacher. But not for long. Both of the students broke the Teacher's only rule, and He threw them out of the classroom. Ever after, all students were prone to break rules, and they all had to study in an imperfect environment.

Only the Teacher remained perfect. He provided a way for his students to want to do right, and He ordained education as a means to help them do right. But the fallen students thought they knew the best way to educate themselves—apart from the Master Teacher. And thus began the battle between secular education and Christian education.

Christian education began in the Garden of Eden—a fact not often cited by education historians but one substantiated by Scripture." [2]

The roots of religious education were evident in early America as those who arrived sought expression of their religious freedoms. Schools in early America did not separate God from the educational equation, and our founding fathers, many of whom were God-fearing men, believed that the Bible played an important role in education. Students learned to read using stories based clearly on biblical truth. Copies of the "Ten Commandments" hung on the classroom walls. A Bible was on the teacher's desk. Class sessions were opened with prayer and Bible devotions. Teachers taught biblical truths and sought to live by them. Communities held teachers accountable for their example to the children.

Major colleges and universities, including Harvard, Princeton, and Yale, were founded on Christian principles. Students of these colleges were required to sign statements of faith in Christ and attend prayer meetings and chapel services.

During the early days of our nation, the majority of public schools, including the colleges and universities, began with a strong religious element and continued to operate that way for some time. The 1647 School Law was based on the Old Deluder Satan Act passed in Massachusetts, which required the teaching, reading and writing of Scriptures to children in a school setting. This formed the basis of what is today known as a public school and the main purpose was to teach children the Scriptures. The belief was that Satan wanted to keep people in ignorance of the Scriptures, so that they would remain in bondage because of the lack of true knowledge.

However, as learning became more available, it also became more secularized, and Scripture lost its central place in most schools. The religious influence that so predominately saturated education in early America was slowly cut away by movements such as humanistic philosophy, modernism, individualism, and intellectualism. The idea of the separation of church and state was pushed which forced true Christianity out of most schools.

Before World War II, various parochial schools, including Catholic, Lutheran, Mennonite, and Amish schools, were in operation, but that was it. When Christian parents began to realize how much their children were being affected by the increasingly secular, humanistic public schools, they began to look for alternatives. They wanted schools with moral standards and discipline as well as a distinctive, biblical, Christ-centered approach in every subject. Pastors challenged congregations to provide Christian schools for the children so that the influence of the Bible teaching of home and church would not be nullified. Slowly, the modern Christian school movement gained momentum.

In 1920, the National Union of Christian Schools was created to promote what was called parent society schools in the Midwestern parts of the country. As a result of this by 1946, the National Association of Christian Schools (NACS) was formed and in 1974, this became the National Christian School Education Association. In 1978, this turned into the Association of Christian Schools International (ACSI), which is now the governing body that oversees evangelical schools in America and overseas.

Between 1920 and 1960 approximately 150 independent evangelical Christian schools existed. Approximately 12,000 Christian schools were founded between the mid 1960s and the 1990s after the courts banished Bible reading and prayer in the public schools. All across the United States, faithful people were planting Christian schools, thousands of which continue today.

However, the age-old battle between Christian education and secular education still continues today, and many are wondering where Christian education is headed in the future. For Christian education to thrive, pastors must continue to teach congregations its importance. Universities must train quality Christian teachers. Christian textbook publishers must produce thoroughly biblical, educationally sound materials. And Christian educators must get these truths and resources into the hands and minds of the students.

Proverbs 3:5-6 says, "Trust in the Lord with all your heart and lean not on your own understanding; in all your ways acknowledge him, and he will make your paths straight." [3] As educational institutions lean more on their own understanding, the divide continues to increase between a Christian worldview and progressive education. There has never before been a greater need for Christian education in our country.

The imparting of moral principles is integrated into the fabric of education whether taught or caught. A true "Christ in Education" experience places the emphasis on our Creator and His Creation in the educational process and combines that with a distinct Christian environment, modeling what is taught. This education can take place at the local church, Christian School, home-school, or in a Godly home. Whatever the case, "Christ in Education" doesn't just simply happen. A true "Christ in Education" experience must be a conscious effort.

God often emphasizes the influence of teachers upon students. In Luke 6:40, Christ says that every student, when fully trained, will be like his teacher. In Ephesians 6:4, He instructs fathers to bring up their children "in the nurture and admonition of the Lord." Then in John 14:6 Christ is identified as the source of all truth. As followers of Christ we must take every opportunity to make God more familiar to our children. We must make the most of every chance to involve Christ in education, whether at home, school, or church.

Many parents struggle financially to keep their children in Christian Schools. Why do they make these sacrifices? Why does a parent give of his/her own time and resources to home-school his/her child? Why does the Sunday School teacher volunteer time and energy every week? Simply put, the words in Ephesians are being lived out in their lives.

The challenge that faces Christian Educators is to hold fast to the foundational reasons they committed to this great cause. Christian educators make an indelible impact on lives for Christ. They help shape a biblical worldview in their students. What can have greater impact? What can be more important?

Richard J. Edlin summarized the core values of a Christian philosophy of education including Scripture references for each value. [4]

Core Value	Biblical Foundation	Affirmations
Centrality of the Bible	Proverbs 3:1 Psalm 119 John 17:6-19 Colossians 3:16	The Bible, God's written Word is preeminent in the life of the Christian. Divinely inspired and inerrant; it is authoritative for all of life, including the life of the Christian school.
A Biblical Worldview	Acts 17:16-34 Colossians 2:8 Joshua 1:8-9 Hebrews 1:1-2	Education is never neutral. Christian education must ensure that students learn about the world and their place and tasks in it from the perspective of a biblical worldview.

The Importance of Parents	Deuteronomy 6:4-9 Psalm 78:1-7 Ephesians 6:1-4	God has given parents the primary responsibility for the nurture of their children. The Christian school partners with parents to assist them in carrying out this responsibility.
The Importance of Teachers	Luke 6:39-40 Colossians 2:6-8 1 Timothy 4:6-11	Christian schools will fail without teachers who clearly understand, teach, and live from the perspective of a radical biblical worldview. Schools need to offer their teachers sustained, biblically authentic professional development.
Nurture in the Christian School	Psalm 8 Ephesians 2:10 Ephesians 4:20-24 Philippians 1:3-11	Children are gifted image bearers, but they are impacted by the Fall and need redemption in Christ. The school should help them discover God's peace and purpose for themselves and their world as stewards responsible to Him.
Responsive Discipleship and the Christian School	Luke 14:25-33 Jeremiah 29:7 Ephesians 3:13-19	Christian education does not just promote personal growth, it equips young people to share God's dynamic message of hope and peace in Christ, in every vocation and activity, to a lost and forlorn generation.

Core Value One: The Centrality of the Bible

A Christian school to be truly Christian must be established on the foundation of God, the creator, who has made Himself known through an authoritative and trustworthy Bible, and of Jesus Christ His Son, the Savior of the world. The foundation of Christian education must start with the Bible and the curriculum must be based on the Bible's code of absolute truth. The resulting biblical perspective on knowledge will involve much more than an understanding of ideas. True knowledge in biblical terms is not attained until it is lived out in the lives of teachers and students. Truth is found most fully in the person and work of the living Word, Jesus Christ. Jesus did not come to just tell us about the truth or give us true words, He is the truth.[5] A Christian school's curriculum must start with this declaration and should bring its students to a deeper knowledge of it. Christian schools must help students use God's word to develop perspectives on reality that are biblically authentic and personally owned, and that will help them to glorify God and live for Him in all they do.

Core Value Two: Biblical Worldview

Christian educators share the awesome responsibility of helping students develop the kind of worldview that leads to holy and responsible life choices. Such a duty demands that educators themsleves learn to think biblically and then to effectively communicate that ability to the sudents. A biblical worldview influences us to live the life God intended for us to live. The aim of Christian educatation is to produce adults who have woven their moral and spiritual lives out of a worldview based on biblical values.[6]

To develop a Christian worldview one must begin with Scripture. Kenneth O. Gangel writes, "It is from the Word of God that we receive special revelation concerning the nature of God, humankind, ultimate reality, goodness and life expectations. While all people have access to general revelation (through the study of God's creation) and to the world's accumulated knowledge, only Christians accept the Bible as our source for the ultimate answers to life. While all systems of philosophy require a measure of faith, a belief in Scripture provides the most internally consistent system on which to build a moral and purposefull life." [7] We believe as Christians that God has given us "everything we need for life and godliness through our knowledge of him who called us by his own glory and goodness" [8]

The premise of Christian education is that all truth is God's truth. By this we mean that all genuine truth can ultimately be traced back to God as its source. "Since the God of revelation is also the God of creation, the true relationship between natural and special revelation begins in the foundation of absolute truth." [9] Christians realize that the "real world" is that which maintains God at its center. They know that God has a new heaven in preparation, so our values reflect eternal outcomes rather than exclusively earthbound ones. [10]

Christian educators must teach their students to use biblical principles as a framework from which to address life's questions, both practical and eternal. In Christian education the faculty and administration must establish the theological and academic framework for the communication of truth. Christian education must include a view of oneself as totally dependent on the work of Christ for both salvation and sanctification.

Personal values are associated with a biblical worldview. A biblical worldview incorporates a belief in the sanctity of life from conception to death leading believers to work for the common good. Believers are also warned that we cannot serve both God and money and that life does not consist in the abundance of things. While money and possessions are not wrong in themselves, "the love of money is the root of all evil." [11] Therefore, believers are warned against covetousness and materialism.

Another personal value associated with a biblical worldview is family. God established the family as the first human institution.[12] Realizing that children represent the next generation of history, Christians share a deep concern for the care and proper instruction of children. Jesus shows His value of children in Luke 18.

The responsibilities of both a worker and a master are also evident in Scripture and are included in a biblical worldview.

Stewardship is another personal value included in a biblical worldview. God holds all people accountable for the resources entrusted to them, which include money and material possessions as well as personal resources such as time, energy, talents, labor, and intelligence. Recognizing that God is the Author of all good and perfect gifts, we endeavor as Christians to be responsible stewards of the resources entrusted to us. We were also given the responsibility to be caretakers of God's world.

Christians are to gather for the study of God's Word, prayer, ministry, and mutual encouragement. Therefore it is important for Christians to attend a Bible teaching church on a regular basis.

Christian educators teaching from a biblical worldview affect the whole student, not just the intellect. Students must learn not only what the Scriptures teach, but also how to live daily in accordance with a biblical worldview.

Core Value Three: Parents

Parents have the God given responsibility for the education of their children. The Christian school partners with the parents to assist with this responsibility. Therefore classrooms should be open environments where parents are encouraged to observe and participate in a non-disruptive manner. Before parents enroll their children in a Christian school they need adequate nurture in a biblical pattern of schooling. The school should provide a seminar for parents of prospective students that explores the radical socially nonconformist purpose and character of the school. Parents

carry out their biblical mandate by ensuring that the policies
and procedures of the school conform to biblical patterns and by
involving themselves in appropriate ways in the life of the school.

Core Value Four: Teachers

Besides parents, teachers are often the most influential adults
in the lives of a child. In Luke 6:40 Jesus says that the student
when fully trained will be like his teacher. Therefore it is vital that
Christian schools hire teachers who have a vibrant walk with Christ,
a passion for teaching and competence in their field. Teachers must
receive on going biblically based professional development. It is
vital for teachers to know the Bible, so Bible seminars must also be
provided. In fact teacher contracts should require them to commit
themselves to such training.

Teachers have gifts and abilities appropriate to their calling.
Schools should be structured in a manner that allows them to
exercise their talents in a God-honoring way. Teachers in Christian
schools not only teach, but also provide a positive role model.
Relationships are at the heart of the Christian gospel, and they
are at the heart of Christian nurture within the Christian school.
In 1 Thessalonians 2:8 Paul blends the twin aspects of truth in
instruction and godly interaction with students.

Core Value Five: Nurture in the Christian School

A biblical worldview gives the educator a wonderful perspective
in the children, whose ultimate worth is found in the fact that they
are made in God's image. As God's image bearer, each child has a
unique set of gifts and talents. The school should help the children
and their families identify and develop these gifts and talents.

In recent decades research has shed new light on such issues as multiple intelligences and learning styles, and knowing about these enables Christian educators to respond appropriately to each child's uniqueness.

As God's image bearers, students also have the need to make moral choices and to be held accountable for them. Students must learn about the world from a biblical worldview and their place and task within the world.

Students are not just created in God's image; they are also deeply scarred by the Fall and impacted by sin. True nurture in the Christian school will acknowledge this reality. Discipline should not be separated from nurture but should focus on truth, confession, and restoration, using a model of discipleship.

Core Value Six: Responsive Discipleship

Christian schools should be equipping students as they come to know the King of kings, to be His ambassadors in the world, seeking to bring His peace into all of life. This is responsive discipleship.

Richard J. Edlin writes that Graduates of Christian schools are "living" report cards for the school. "If Christian schools are to receive a passing grade, their graduates should be evident in the world, challenging the idolatrous status quo and offering an alternative view that is biblically authentic and that genuinely seeks the welfare of the city they live in." [13]

Chapter Two:
Christian School Institutions

Deuteronomy 6:4-9 "Here, O Israel: The Lord our God, the Lord is one. Love the Lord your God with all your heart and with all your soul and with all your strength. These commandments that I give you today are to be upon your hearts. Impress them on your children. Talk about them when you sit at home and when you walk along the road, when you lie down and when you get up. Tie them as symbols on your hands and bind them on your foreheads. Write them on the doorframes of your houses and on your gates." [14]

The need for Christian education is so great. We must remember that God gives parents the responsibility to educate their children. Deuteronomy 6:4-9 speaks of God's requirement for the education of His children. Many parents enroll their children in schools and allow the schools to assist them in educating their children.

However, the government schools of today are not the answer. Douglas Wilson writes extensively against government schools. He writes, "The Word of God and the word of man are at odds and mutually exclusive. They can never agree on the facts of reality on any point. It is the mutual exclusiveness of these two positions that makes the provision of a specifically Christian education vital. Sending our children to a government school to be educated by humanists is a denial of our faith." [15] Douglas also points out that Christian parents have a moral obligation to keep their children out of government schools because of the agnostic form of education received in these schools. [16]

In Psalm 78:5-8 we see the importance of covenant education. When that education fails, the terms of the covenant are not kept over the course of generations. "All of life is under the authority of God's revealed Word, and children are to be taught in terms of this comprehensive authority of all time." [17]

There are many different types of Christian schools and other methods of receiving a Christian education. Some Christian schools are independent of any other organization. Some Christian churches have started schools for families in their congregation as a ministry of their church. Many parents choose to keep their children at home and teach them using Christian home school programs. Some Christian schools support parents who are home schooling their children by allowing the children to enroll in a course at their school, or by providing tutorial services for the students.

Independent Christian schools are not associated with any particular church and are free from any particular denomination. Students who attend such a school come from many different Christian churches. The school's governing board is independent of any other organization.

Other Christian schools are linked with a particular church. The school may be one of the church's ministries. Many students enrolled in the school attend the sponsoring church, but such a school often enrolls students from other churches as well. Some schools grant a discount for parents who are tithing members of the sponsoring church.

One choice parents have as mentioned above is to home school their children. There are many programs available to assist the parents with this task. Some Christian schools, such as, The King School in Lake Luzerne, NY have a home school affiliation program and offer support services for parents who home school their children. Home-schooled students may even be able to sign up for one or two courses offered at the school and may participate in the school's sports programs.

Liberty University, the world's largest evangelical college, offers online home school courses for elementary, middle school, and high school programs as well as for college level courses. Another online high school is Oaks Christian Online School. A Beka is a very popular program for Christian home schooling. Other Christian home school programs include BJU Press, Bob Jones, Alpha Omega Publications, Sonlight, Learning by Grace, Christian Liberty Academy School Systems, and many others. Many parents search textbook companies and choose texts for their children from a variety of companies.

Some Christian schools are accredited and others are not. Accreditation is used to assure quality in schools and educational institutions. Accreditation is a voluntary, non-governmental process of review and evaluation. Such a process requires an educational institution to meet certain defined standards or criteria as set forth by the accrediting body. These standards change from region to region; they also change with time. Each accrediting body sets its own standards.

Schools that are not accredited have a certain degree of freedom in designing their schools structure, philosophy, teaching modalities, and evaluation criteria. They are not restricted by requirements established by traditional licensing or other accrediting organizations. It is vital that Christian schools stay away from any kind of licensing or accreditation that might prevent them from teaching from a Christian worldview or weaken their ability to train students to be effective servants of Christ. Christian schools must strive to be pleasing to God, not man and they must be concerned about honoring Christ and serving Him.

Christian accreditation is advantageous however in that it assures a level of competency. Prospective students and their parents will be able to see that the school meets certain standards. The parents and students can be assured of the quality of education that is provided by the educational institution. Accrediting organizations assist schools to reach accreditation standards and help schools to strive for improvement in an orderly and systematic way. The accreditation process brings a vigorous dynamic into the school by engaging every staff member in a process of organizational appraisal. The process of accreditation and school improvement can be very rigorous, however, when scheduled properly, it is not overwhelming and the end results are well worth the investment.

Accreditation is a voluntary process validated by peer review and involving systematic self-evaluation against nationally accepted standards. Usually the process includes five main steps: An application process, candidate status, a self-study process, a team visit for validation by peer review, and finally a commission decision by the accrediting organization. There are many Christian accrediting organizations available: Association of Christian Schools International, National Association of Private Schools, Association of Classical and Christian Schools, The American Association of Christian Schools, The International Christian Accrediting Association, Transnational Association of Christian Colleges and Schools, and many others.

The self-study will include evaluation of every aspect of the school including the facilities, staff, the academic program, the spiritual emphasis, and business practices. Even if a school chooses not to seek accreditation a self-study would be a very valuable tool for self-improvement of the school.

The decision to attain accredited status produces more total school benefit than any other action that a school can take. Curriculum quality is strengthened, school policies are refined, student achievement enhanced, and future directions strengthened. Without accreditation the attainment of overall excellence for a Christian school is very difficult.

Accreditation should be viewed as an ongoing process of school-wide improvement and development through which a school or program strives for educational and spiritual excellence. It is a process of recognizing and assessing schools and programs against accepted standards of performance, integrity, and quality. A Christian accreditation process will reflect upon the spiritual aspects of each component of the school as well as evaluate the educational quality and integrity of the organization.

The accrediting process through a Christian organization will address the distinctive of the faith-based program of a Christian school and the components that make an eternal impact on children, students, and families. It will also addresses the issues demonstrating that the school is true to its own statements of philosophy, mission, and goals and that it is meeting the standards of quality and effectiveness. Therefore a Christian school should examine the requirements of various accreditation organizations and seriously consider engaging in the accreditation process.

Chapter Three:
An Academic Program with
An Emphasis On Biblical Values

Psalm 78:1-8 "O my people, hear my teaching; listen to the words of my mouth. I will open my mouth in parables, I will utter things hidden from of old—things we have heard and known, things our fathers have told us. We will not hide them from their children; we will tell the next generation the praiseworthy deeds of the Lord, his power, and the wonders he has done. He decreed statutes for Jacob and established the law in Israel, which he commanded our forefathers to teach their children, so the next generation would know them, even the children yet to be born, and they in turn would tell their children. Then they would put their trust in God and would not forget his deeds but would keep his commands. They would not be like their forefathers—a stubborn and rebellious generation, whose hearts were not loyal to God, whose spirits were not faithful to him." [18]

In order to be a true Christian school there must be a spiritual emphasis throughout the entire academic program. The school must be teaching a biblical worldview. Charles Colson and Nancy Pearcey challenge Christian educational institutions with the following statement:

"Christian education is not simply a matter of starting class with Bible reading and prayer, then teaching subjects out of secular textbooks. It consists of teaching everything, from science and mathematics to literature and the art's, within the framework of an integrated biblical worldview. It means teaching students to relate every academic discipline to God's truth and his self-revelation in Scripture, while detecting and critiquing nonbiblical worldview assumptions." [19]

Lois E. LeBar states in Education That Is Christian, "Action is always carried out by means of some method. If we aren't doing His work in the Spirit by His methods, we're doing it in the flesh by our own methods. The Lord's work done in the Lord's way will have the Lord's supply." [20] This illustrates how important it is for every staff member of the school to be in right relationship with the Lord. The staff members must be students of the Bible, have a consistent prayer life, and be actively involved in a Bible teaching evangelical church. LeBar goes on to say "Although the Bible was not written as a textbook of educational philosophy or method, the believer who seeks 'buried educational treasure' will be richly rewarded. These treasures are not grouped by categories and openly displayed for the casual observer, but are 'hidden' for the earnest seeker who is willing to dig for them." [21]

Key questions to ask when considering the curriculum of a Christian school include the following. What are the aims and worldview foundations of Christian school programs? How do you plan a yearly overview? How do you design and adapt unit plans for classrooms? How do you select suitable classroom resources? How do you implement curriculum change effectively?

In a Christian approach to curriculum, students learn about God's creation and how humans have unfolded it, and how God calls us to respond as disciples of Jesus Christ. A Christian approach fosters students' positive response and responsibility to God, their fellow humans, and society. The Christian curriculum takes the students on a journey that deepens understanding of God's revelation, both in His Word and in His world, and its implications for life.

Harro Van Brummelen provides a helpful chart in his essay about curriculum design. [22]

Aims of the Christian School Curriculum and Related Questions

Aims of the Curriculum	Questions for Justifying Curriculum Choices
Overall Aim: To become committed to Jesus Christ and to a Christian way of life, able and willing to serve God, neighbor, and society.	Does the curriculum: • Teach content from a perspective that is faithful to Scripture? • Enhance understandings and abilities for exercising responsible and responsive discipleship? • Consider biblical values and encourage students to form dispositions and commitments based on them?
To unfold the basis, framework, and implications of a Christian vision of life.	Does the curriculum: • Help students know and experience a Christian worldview and its implications for life in society? • Encourage students to choose and commit themselves to a biblical way of life?
To learn about God's world and how humans have responded to God's mandate to take care of the earth.	Does the curriculum: • Familiarize students with our Christian and Western cultural heritage? • Address meaningful and significant current issues? • Show the wonder of God's creation? Show how humans have unfolded as well as abused His world? Show what it means to live according to God's intent for His creation?
To develop and apply the concepts, abilities, and creative gifts that enable students to have a transformational impact on culture for Jesus Christ.	Does the curriculum: • Develop students' diverse abilities, taking into account their stages of development and their different learning styles? • Ask students to create products, procedures, and theories that unfold God's reality and develop their insights, abilities, and dispositions? • Encourage students to use their learning to contribute to life both inside and outside of school? Help them to become servant leaders who support each other to promote the lordship of Christ in all areas of life?

To discern and confront the idols of our time: materialism, hedonism, scientism, relativism, and other "isms" in which people place their faith in something other than God.	Does the curriculum: • Make students aware of, and able to critique, the shared meanings of our culture? • Foster understanding and discernment of key trends and issues in society? • Help students promote the positive and confront the negative characteristics of our culture?

This chart will prove helpful when designing a school curriculum and also to evaluate an existing curriculum. [23] Harro Van Brummelen also discusses the key elements of a biblically based worldview. He points out that the history of the world can be described in four main epochs, each with a special God-given injunction and each with particular implications for curriculum design.

1. **God's creation of the world, including humans in His image.** God told Adam and Eve to be fruitful, to rule over the earth, and to tend and take care of God's garden (Gen. 1:28 and 2:15). This is known as God's Creation Mandate. God called humans to develop the possibilities of His creation and to be stewards of His creation, to enable everything in God's world to fulfill its intended functions. The fall into sin did not negate that call, even though sin will continue to undermine human efforts until Christ's return. God calls our students to learn about, use, and value mathematical, physical, and biological entities and theories. He calls them to be involved in advancing civilization on the basis of biblical norms. They explore God's guidelines for family life, business law, government, communication, the uses of technology, and aesthetics. The curriculum helps answer the question: What is God's intention for the particular area of creation or culture that we are investigating?

2. **The fall into sin.** We live in a self-centered, not a God-centered world. The school's curriculum should address how human disobedience and sin has distorted God's purpose. How have humans deviated from God's original intentions? Once we see how God's intent for His good creation has been warped by sin and evil, our response is to live lives of love for God and His world. [24] Love is the key to being transformed by the renewing of our minds so that we no longer conform to the pattern of this world. The curriculum must help students discern how personal and societal sin affects morality, government, crime, warfare, economics, interpersonal relationships, communications, the media, and our environment. It also should encourage students to use their gifts in service to and love for God and neighbor, to develop the "mind of Christ". [25] Praise and thanksgiving should be built into the curriculum. Also the school should include content that deals with issues in our society where agape love can make a difference, students use diverse gifts to help each other, and apply learning in service projects.

3. **God's redemption in Jesus Christ.** How can we, through Christ's work of redemption, restore, at least in part, the love, righteousness, and justice that God intended for the world? How can the curriculum lead students into a deeper understanding of experience in, and commitment to a Christian way of life? After His resurrection, Jesus added to the Creation Mandate both the Great Commission and the Great Commandment. [26] Jesus enjoins us to make disciples (not just converts) of all nations (not just individuals). Disciples are people who base their thinking, words, and deeds on the principles Jesus taught us. Jesus makes clear that we are to teach people to obey everything he has commanded. Curriculum leads students to cherish

and promote humility, self-sacrifice, mercy, peace, justice, righteousness, truthfulness, faithfulness, and generosity— and to avoid legalism and hypocrisy, and to explore responsible Christian responses to the influence of sin. The curriculum of the Christian school should also help students investigate what it means to be Christ's ambassadors wherever God places them, using insights, abilities, and value-based attitudes in God-glorifying ways.

4. **Fulfillment of God's promise.** How can we instill in our students a sense of hope, strength, and courage despite the many problems and struggles they face? We must reject the idea of the innate goodness of humans. The Bible makes it clear that we are tainted with sin. The curriculum should leave the students with a sense of hope. God's goodness is still evident in our world and we look forward to full restoration of God's intent for His creation. The school's curriculum should promote what is just and loving, both personally and together as a Christian community.

Throughout the curriculum the school should strive to develop the students' sense of responsibility, combining high expectations with love, encouragement, and support. The staff should model biblical values, give reasons for them, and introduce cases that lead students to consider how such values apply in specific circumstances. For example, in literature choose selections that promote respect and compassion. In social studies discuss questions of social justice as well as value dilemmas faced by historical figures. In science promote precise and truthful reporting of data. In math teach students to research and plot morally significant social trends. Teach the importance of accuracy in math, and clarity in communication.

The curriculum should integrate Scripture and scriptural

principles into every aspect of the student's education at every grade level. It should cultivate wisdom rather than just teaching facts and skills; developing a love for discovery and learning as a primary objective. The curriculum must utilize subjects such as language arts, history, science, math, theology, philosophy, art, music, and physical education in a manner based upon the developmental stages of the student. Finally it is very important that the curriculum is designed to equip students to read critically, express themselves effectively in writing and speech, and to reason acutely as they develop a broad knowledge base across the traditional academic disciplines.

Developing A General School Schedule

The administrator should develop a general school schedule. He may appoint a task force of teachers to work out a school wide scope-and-sequence chart and to recommend basic resources. Once these are approved the teachers will write a yearly outline for their courses and then develop and adapt unit plans. Later they will plan day-to-day lessons. The teachers should evaluate their plans and see if they line up with the school's vision and aims. Do the lessons uphold a biblical worldview and vision? Do the lessons help students become responsive and responsible disciples? Do the lessons employ varied learning strategies suited for the class? Do the lessons meet the expectations of the school as well as other official standards?

Yearly course outlines should list the schedule, topics, content, goals, the main concept, understandings and values, key skills to be learned and major student assessment strategies. The time allotment should reflect a balanced consideration of all topics, with no undue repetition between the years. Each topic should contribute to the school's mission and aims

Harro Van Brummelen lists nine steps to planning a classroom unit. [27]

1. Consider the significance and relevance of a topic. There are several questions to consider. How can the topic contribute to the students' understanding of a Christian worldview, biblical values, and our Christian and cultural heritage? How does the topic expand students' previous knowledge and give them insight into significant issues? How can the topic meet students' learning needs and lead to worthwhile skill development?

2. Brainstorm ideas. A good way to begin is to ask four worldview questions. What is God's intention for the particular area of creation or culture that we are investigating? How has God's purpose been distorted by human disobedience and sin? How have humans deviated from God's original intent? Are there ways in which we can restore, at least in part, the love, righteousness, and justice that God intended for the world? How can we instill in our students a sense of hope, strength, and courage despite the many problems and struggles they face? Then consider key values, skills, and activities that you would like to include in the unit.

3. Formulate your unit theme and focus thematic statement. This will be the overall aim and approach of the unit. It includes the basic understandings, concepts, skills, values, dispositions, and commitments you want students to acquire. Also develop a set of intended learning outcomes. The outcomes are more specific than the thematic statement. The outcomes identify desired results of learning and provide direction and balance. At this point the curriculum writer should also formulate three or four guiding questions.

4. Design and choose learning activities. Check that each

learning activity contributes to one or more learning outcomes. The range of learning activities should be suitable for students with different ability levels and learning styles. All students should have opportunities for involvement and personal responses. The activities should promote the learning of meaningful concepts and enduring understandings, worthwhile abilities and thinking skills, and important values, and commitments. The introductory activity must be motivational and the concluding activity must review the main theme, understandings, and values.

5. Incorporate external standards. Check for state guidelines or standards. Some state guidelines and standards will be rejected. They may contradict God's directives. Other standards, however, will help the students. Also check for guidelines and standards from Christian school accreditation organizations.

6. Plan a schedule. Decide how many weeks the unit will take. Check the yearly outline. Decide how much time you will spend on the unit each day. Make a time chart to keep yourself on track.

7. Select suitable resources. Choose textbooks and resources carefully. Find out what commitments, values, priorities, and goals are stated or assumed in the materials. Are there any overt or subtle biases in the materials? Do the materials promote biblical norms for ethical, economic, aesthetic, and family life? What topics and issues does the resource consider important and do these match your priorities and goals? Does the resource support different types of learning activities, encouraging students to be thoughtful, responsive, and creative? Is the level of difficulty suitable?

8. Plan student assessment. Align learning outcomes, activities, products, and assessment strategies. Use varied

strategies.

9. Review the effectiveness of the unit. After the unit is
    taught evaluate it. Did you accomplish the unit's intended
    outcomes? Did the students grasp the key themes and
    enduring understandings? Which learning strategies were
    successful? Which fell short of your expectations? Were the
    resources appropriate? Was the student assessment suitable
    and helpful? What should be changed next time? Make
    notes and put them with the unit file.

The curriculum should include courses that will teach skills to
prepare students for what God has planned. These include Biblical
knowledge, reading, oral communication, mathematics, technical
skills, higher order thinking and reasoning, discernment, and social
skills. Each school day should begin with a devotional period of
Scripture reading with a discussion of the reading followed with
prayer. In some Christian schools the students report directly to
their classrooms where the school day begins with pledges to the
American Flag, the Christian Flag, and the Bible and then a period
of Scripture reading with discussion and prayers. In other Christian
schools everyone reports to a large assembly. The students sit in
class groups with their teachers. The assembly opens with the
pledges followed by devotion and prayer led by the administrator
before the students are dismissed to their classes. Once a week
this assembly is replaced by a chapel service led by a local pastor.
After the students settle in their desks in the classroom the teacher
reviews the Scripture reading from the assembly or chapel service
and opens class with prayer. Then the students begin their seatwork
assignments that are listed on the board while the teacher takes
attendance and handles some administrative tasks before beginning
the first reading group.

Usually the morning classes focus on the language arts. This includes reading, grammar, spelling, writing, literature, and speech. In the afternoon there will be classes in Bible, mathematics, science, social studies, art, music, and physical education. Many Christian schools include Latin or other languages in their curriculum. This is especially true of classical Christian schools. I have provided a sample schedule at the end of this chapter. Of course adjustments can be made so every class doesn't have foreign language, physical education, music, and art at the same time, especially if you have special teachers and/or special rooms for these subjects.

Evaluating and Choosing Curriculum Materials

The next consideration is obtaining resources for teaching the various subjects. Several publishing companies publish Christian textbooks. "A Beka" is not only used for home schooling, but is used in many Christian schools today. Other companies that publish Christian textbooks include Christian Liberty Press, BJU Press, Alpha Omega Publications, and many others.

The administrator of the school should appoint a textbook committee to examine textbooks from several companies. It is imperative that the textbooks do not teach anything contrary to a Christian worldview and that they provide for high academic standards. Nancy Ferguson has written a book to assist with choosing and developing curriculum for Christian Education. [28] Her suggestions are written for considering curriculum for Bible lessons, but the ideas can be adapted to consider other subject areas as well. It would be beneficial for the administrator and faculty to study this book when seeking to develop the curriculum for a school. She sets forth six key elements that should be considered when developing curriculum. [29] I have adapted these for the use in Christian schools.

Key 1 is a statement of purpose or goal. This should include the purpose or goals of the school and the purpose and goals for each subject and grade area. Key 2 concerns the school's understanding of the Bible and how it should be used in the educational programs. Key 3 provides an overview and summary of all of the settings for education in the school. Key 4 addresses the content to be taught in the educational programs. Key 5 defines the role of the teachers. Key 6 defines the role of the students.

Once the six key elements are apparent the curriculum committee will be ready to evaluate purchased curriculum or to organize to develop their own curriculum resources. The committee should begin each meeting in prayer and the committee members should be encouraged to pray daily about the school's curriculum. Then the committee will need to study the school's mission statement and goals or write them if the school has not already written these. Next, they need to identify the elements of the school's educational program that will be used as a foundation statement for decisions the school will be making about curricula.

The administration of the school should list the subjects that will be taught at each grade level. Bible, language arts and literature, math, science, social studies, art, music, and physical education are subjects that are taught in most Christian schools. Classical Christian schools teach Latin and many Christian schools have added foreign language and computer courses to their curriculum. Then the scope and sequence for each subject should be listed for each grade level.

It is most important that the teachers open class each day with a devotional study and prayer. There should be a chapel service led by a local pastor once a week. Local pastors should be encouraged to make frequent visits to the school.

When examining curriculum resources the administrator should look for materials that teach from a biblical worldview and are more current, challenging, and engaging. Another point to keep in mind when searching for curriculum materials is to find materials that provide for teaching that will give students continual longing to know more about the wonderful world God has created. The administrator should then form a committee of teachers to evaluate textbooks and materials and make recommendations for the administrator's and board approval.

Many schools make the mistake of making decisions about printed resources on the basis of appearance and cost. They want materials that are colorful, that have extras such as craft kits and student workbooks, and that are affordable. During the selection process administrators and textbook selection committees need to refrain from using such criteria and choose a curriculum resource by drawing on the schools six key elements.

Curriculum resources created and sold by publishing companies, both denominational and independent, are all written from certain theological and biblical perspectives. They engage an educational approach that they believe supports those particular perspectives. It is important to know the biblical tradition and educational approach of your school and of the curriculum. The knowledge of both will contribute to the selection of a curriculum resource that will enable you to meet your school's goals.

An important first step in preparing to evaluate published curricula is to identify the theological and educational assumptions and perspectives held by the publisher. Only when you have identified the assumptions within a curriculum will you be able to compare them with the six key elements you have determined that reflect the educational goals and mission of your school.

The first assumption concerns the publishing house's view of what a Christian is and how the Christian faith is nurtured. The purpose of the curriculum needs to support your goals and mission.

The second assumption concerns the publishing house's understanding of Scripture and its role in the life of a Christian. If the resource is at odds with your tradition's understanding of Scripture, then the curriculum will not assist you in reaching your goals. Another helpful clue in identifying a view of Scripture is to determine the versions of the Bible recommended and used in the material. If it is not the version most frequently used within the educational settings and worship of your school, you will probably discover other incompatibilities in biblical assumptions. Look for the following words and phrases in printed resources:
- Bible Truths and Values
- Bible Facts
- Application of Biblical Values to Daily Life

The third assumption publishers will identify are age groups and settings for which the curriculum is written. You will need to examine materials that are appropriate for the age group and for the setting you need. Compare the resources with the information you gathered for Key 3.

The fourth assumption concerns the publishing house's choice for the content of its printed curriculum or the way it chooses to organize the content. It is important that you decide on the content you want to teach rather than having it first determined by the publisher's curriculum.

To identify the content of a curriculum, look for a chart providing the themes, scope and sequence of the materials and the teaching methods used. Such a chart is usually found in the front of the teacher's guide. A review of this chart will enable you to compare the scope of the content and organization of it with the content you want to teach. Again, it is important to ask whether the content will help you to reach the overall goal of your educational ministry.

Assumption 5 deals with certain understandings about how people learn their faith. These assumptions become explicit in the teaching methods used. They include an understanding of the roles of both teacher and learner. The educational concepts you identified in keys 5 and 6 should match the educational theory of the purchased resources.

The best way to evaluate teaching methods and understanding of how people learn their faith is to read through several session plans. Notice what kind of role the teacher or leader plays in these sessions. Is the teacher given a script? Are correct answers provided to questions? What kinds of activities are used to engage the learners? Are the activities much the same, or is there a lot of variety? How are the students involved in the learning process? Also read the objectives or purpose of each lesson and think about how these stated purposes will enable your students to reach your school's educational goals.

By matching the publisher assumptions with the six key elements you have identified for your school you will be able to find a curriculum that enriches your educational program. Such a match will strengthen the total school program and will enable you to reach the goals you have set.

Publishers will usually provide examination copies of their teacher guides, student texts, and any other materials that go along with their curriculum. Be sure to have materials from four to eight publishers available before the selection committee meets.

Prior to the first meeting of the selection committee either the administrator or the committee chairman should also do a cost analysis for each curriculum series you will present to the committee for evaluation. Prepare a Curriculum Cost Assessment for each of the curriculum series that you have chosen.

For each curriculum series that you are considering, include the detailed information about costs for the number of teacher guides, student books, and classroom resources you will need. Have copies of the cost assessment available for each committee member. Even though the decision about curriculum should not be made based on price, it certainly can be a factor. Knowing the prices of curriculum may enable the committee to choose between their top two final choices. A sample format for the Curriculum Cost Assessment form is provided at the end of this chapter.

When the committee meets to evaluate the curriculum materials from several publishers you should set up the room with a separate small table for each publishing company. Set up a table in the center of the room with chairs for each committee member. Provide each committee member with Curriculum Evaluation Forms for each publishing company. (A sample form is provided the end of this chapter.)

Open the meeting with prayer. It is important to pray for guidance and wisdom that God will direct their choices. Then explain that during the meeting the group will be examining several resources. Review the six key elements of the school that the committee had previously identified and explain the evaluation form. Point out the Curricula on the tables around the room and ask the members to complete a Curriculum Evaluation form for each publishing company that they evaluate. Ask them to give each curriculum an overall rating for consistency with the school's educational mission and goals. Give the committee members time to examine the materials.

Gather everyone back together. As a group walk around the tables holding the curriculum materials and ask those who reviewed the curriculum to share their evaluations. On a piece of newsprint, create a master list. Record the name of each curriculum and all the numerical ratings it received from the evaluators. As the group moves around to hear the evaluation for each curriculum, add the name and ratings to the newsprint. At the end of the time, you will have a list of the curriculum and the scores each received. Add the combined ratings for each sample and divide by the number of reviewers to find its average rating.

Identify the two or three resources that ranked highest and take them to the center table. Pass out the cost assessments you completed earlier for these curricula. Discuss the costs of the curriculum plus the strengths and weaknesses of each curriculum. Discuss how adaptations could possibly be made to overcome the weaknesses of each curriculum.

Ask the group whether they are ready to make the decision about which of these resources will best strengthen and enable your educational goals to be reached. If you already have a consensus, then the decision is made. If a decision is not clear, take a vote. Based on this vote, make a final choice about the curriculum and prepare a proposal for board action.

Give thanks to everyone at the meeting and close in prayer.

Writing Curriculum Matierials

Sometimes you will need to produce your own curriculum materials or make adaptations to purchased curriculum. The decision to write your own materials requires commitment to a complex, long-term process and should be made only after prayer and careful consideration. Even though writing your own curriculum is both time and energy consuming, it can also bring a great deal of satisfaction. It involves the pleasure of seeing teachers ready and eager to teach and learners excited about learning. Those who write curricula often find that their own faith is enriched and deepened through the process of developing resources for others to use. Having materials that enable you to reach your school's goals makes the time and energy spent well worth the effort.

The first step in the process of writing your own printed resources is to determine the educational settings in which you are currently using printed resources and where new resources are needed. Begin by reviewing the information you compiled for Key 3. At that point you completed a list of educational settings in your school and the curriculum used in each setting. Begin by asking for which setting you have been unable to find resources that match your educational goals, the age group, and the Scriptural foundation. Where is the greatest need? It is for this setting that you will want to begin to develop your own curriculum. Begin by deciding whether you will develop resources for all grade levels or concentrate on a single grade level.

Since writing curriculum is complicated and takes much time and energy, it is recommended that you start small. Start with a very narrow focus in terms of age group, theme, and setting. This will give you a chance to try out writing your own resources as well as developing a system to support the creation of your own curriculum. By starting small you will have the opportunity to gauge the time and energy involved, identify people and writing and editing skills within the school, and discover your design and production options.

Writing curriculum is a huge undertaking, and it might not be right for your school. However, if you do decide to write the curriculum it is time to narrow down the theme into a main idea. A main idea states the major ideas and concepts of a passage. Next, read through the main idea and consider the ages of the learners. Ask whether the concepts in the main idea are appropriate for them. You may determine to limit the concepts for younger learners and expand them for older students.

You should create a session planning or lesson plan outline sheet. On this sheet you will record the theme, Bible passage, main idea, goal, outcomes (objectives), supplies, opening, ideas for presenting, exploring and responding to the main idea, and suggestions for closing the lesson. I have provided a sample form at the end of this chapter.

Complete the lesson plan outline as you go along by filling in the theme, Bible passage, and the main idea. This information will be included at the beginning of each session plan. You will use these statements to maintain a consistency between their activities and the main idea.

Now you are ready to focus on the goal and objectives for the lesson. A goal narrows the focus of all the things there are to know or understand about the topic. Goals are written from the perspective of the teacher. They provide the focus for the session and describe the hope, vision, intention, and direction of the session. A goal does not, however, describe specifics about how it will be reached.

Objectives, however, are attainable, specific, and measurable. They describe in concrete terms exactly what the learner will know or be able to do at tend of the session. Teachers should be able to look at the written objectives after a session is completed and know whether the learners reached these outcomes. For example, an objective may read: "Learners will be able to divide a five digit number by a three digit number." The writer's task is to develop sessions in which the students will learn how to divide five digit numbers by three digit numbers. The teacher of these sessions should be able to confirm that the students did indeed learn how to divide such numbers.

The final step in getting ready for writing is to set up an individual session structure or outline that will be used throughout the curriculum. Using the same structure for the sessions will contribute to the ease of both writing and teaching. The structure provides a guide for the movement or flow of the session from introduction to the main idea to the conclusion of the lesson time.

The structure helps the writers by enabling them to ask such things as how to begin, how to connect with learners, and how to close the session. Rather than being a hindrance to creativity, the structure enables writers and teachers to move in a consistent manner through each session.

Each lesson needs an opening, a way to present the main idea, a way to explore the main idea, a method for the students to respond to the main idea, and a meaningful closing.

The opening provides a way to welcome learners into the learning space and into a time of learning. Writers will want to include suggestions for ways to set up the room, ways leaders can engage learners as they arrive, and ways to set the stage for the person or subject to be discussed. This is a time to set the tone for the session.

The presentation for the main idea, whether it is a Bible story, a theological concept, or a moral value begins after the opening. Depending on the age group, the writers have a wide variety of choices about how to present the idea or concept. It needs to be presented clearly so that the learners can understand it and respond as the lesson proceeds.

The writers must also develop ways for learners to explore, interpret, and preserve the main idea. The students will also consider the ways in which the main idea relates or applies to their own lives. A variety of activities in this section of the lesson will keep learners interested and involved.

Next the lesson must invite the learners to make a response to the main idea, concept, or story. This is the way they engage with the concept or idea, relate it to their own experiences and lives, and make a response of some kind, showing their learning. Just as there are a wide variety of ways to present a main idea, there are many ways to invite learners to respond.

The closing pulls all the other parts of the session together. It is a time for the summary of the main idea and celebration of what has been learned and a time to end the lesson in a meaningful way.

Once the curriculum is written and all resources are gathered or created it will be time to train the teachers in the use of the curriculum. If the teachers do not understand the curriculum and/or the resources are not readily available the new curriculum will not be used effectively and all of the hours of work put in by the writers will have been wasted. Implementing the curriculum requires the support of the entire Christian school community. Everyone must be committed to the change. Teachers are at the heart of effective curriculum change. They must support the program's rationale goals, and main features. They must be convinced that the program will benefit learning.

When the curriculum is in place it must be evaluated. Are the program content and learning strategies as well as the resources in harmony with the school's mission and vision? Are the teachers successfully implementing the program? Why or why not? What effect does the program have on students' knowledge, discernments, skills and abilities, values, disposition, and commitments? What impact does the curriculum have? What are the program's strengths and weaknesses? Does it meet quality and quantity standards? Is it up-to-date? What are the results compared to programs in other schools? Do the results justify the costs in time, money, and emotional investment?

On the following pages are some sample forms that may be used or adapted to evaluate and write curriculum.

Sample School Schedule

8:00 Monday – Thursday School Opens with Assembly in the
    Auditorium (Cafeteria)

8:00 Friday Chapel Service

8:30 Students report to classrooms. Prayer and discussion of
    morning devotions.

8:45 Seatwork Assignments (Teacher takes attendance and
    prepares for the day.)

9:00 Language Arts: Reading, Grammar, Spelling, Writing, and
    Speech

10:30 Special Subjects: Music, Computer, Foreign Language,
    P.E., etc. on a rotating basis

11:00 Math

12:00 Lunch

1:00 Bible

2:00 Science/Social Studies

Curriculum Evaluation

Name of Curriculum: _____

Publisher: _____

Educational Philosophy: _____

Age Groups: _____

Setting: _____

_____

_____

Purpose of Curriculum: _____

_____

_____

View of Scripture: _____

_____

_____

Recommended or quoted version of the Bible: _____

_____

_____

Role of Teacher: _____

_____

_____

Role of Student: _____

_____

_____

_____

On a scale of 1 to 5 (with 1 being the lowest) rate this curriculum in its consistency with the purpose of the educational goals of our school.

  1   2   3   4   5

Curriculum Cost Assessment

Name of Curriculum _____

Publisher _____

Age Group _____

Total for Curriculum

Cost for Teacher Guide   Number of Teacher Guides Needed   Total
Cost of Classroom Activity Packs Number of Packs Needed   Total
Cost of Student Books   Number of Students   Total
Cost of Other Resources   Number Needed   Total
Total for Curriculum

Age Group

Cost for Teacher Guide   Number of Teacher Guides Needed   Total
Cost of Classroom Activity Packs Number of Packs Needed   Total
Cost of Student Books   Number of Students   Total
Cost of Other Resources   Number Needed   Total
Total for Curriculum

Age Group

Cost for Teacher Guide   Number of Teacher Guides Needed   Total
Cost of Classroom Activity Packs Number of Packs Needed   Total
Cost of Student Books   Number of Students   Total
Cost of Other Resources   Number Needed   Total
Total for Curriculum

Age Group

Cost for Teacher Guide   Number of Teacher Guides Needed   Total
Cost of Classroom Activity Packs Number of Packs Needed   Total
Cost of Student Books   Number of Students   Total
Cost of Other Resources   Number Needed   Total
Total for Curriculum

Age Group

Cost for Teacher Guide   Number of Teacher Guides Needed   Total
Cost of Classroom Activity Packs Number of Packs Needed   Total
Cost of Student Books   Number of Students   Total
Cost of Other Resources   Number Needed   Total
Total for Curriculum

Lesson Plan Outline

Theme: _____

Bible Passage: _____

Main Idea: _____

_____

_____

Goal: _____

_____

Objectives: _____

_____

_____

_____

Supplies: _____

_____

_____

Opening: _____

_____

_____

Presenting the main idea: _____

_____

_____

_____

Exploring the main idea: _____

_____

_____

_____

Responding to the main idea: _____

_____

_____

Closing: _____

_____

Chapter Four:
Quality Staff and Training

Luke 6:40 (NIV) "A student is not above his teacher, but everyone who is fully trained will be like his teacher." [30]

The Importance of a Quality Staff

The "living" curriculum of a Christian school consists of the teachers whose lives serve as examples of maturing, ministering believers. This "living" curriculum in a Christian school is the key to effective training. In Luke, Jesus taught His disciples "A student is not above his teacher, but everyone who is fully trained will be like his teacher." This "living" curriculum will lead to caring and serving as students learn to make a difference in their world through living the truth and loving their neighbors.

It is imperative that Christian schools provide quality teachers and staff who embody the "living curriculum". They need to live out the principles they want their students to internalize. Being a Biblical role model is a calling of the Christian teacher. Students are very much aware of the spiritual conditions and enthusiasm of their teachers toward the things of God. Students need to see their teachers as living examples of Christians who live out the Christian principles. Besides parents, teachers are often the most influential adults in the lives of children. Christian schools must hire staff members who will not only teach, but who will also provide a positive role model. The strength of the school is the solid faculty who will not only serve the students, but who will serve each other as well. The teachers must show a commitment to teaching to transform character, not just academics. Children learn from the example of parents and teachers who are willing to reach out to those around them, sharing the gospel message, and ministering to people's needs. In this way students will learn to become world Christians. [31]

"The curriculum materials are only an aid for teachers to use. It is the teachers' relationship with Christ and their relationship with learners that best teaches the ways of faith. The training of teachers needs to include not only the resources themselves, but background for the Bible passages, innovative teaching methods, and insight into the learning styles of students. It is important that teachers know the purpose of educational ministry and understand how what they do contributes to that goal." [32]

Teaching in a Christian school is a calling and a ministry that results from knowing God and following His direction. Being a Christian educator is a spiritual ministry that has a passion and a purpose. The teacher is responsible to be a spiritual and an academic role model. Teachers in a Christian school must embrace a biblical worldview. As a spiritual leader, the Christian schoolteacher accepts the authority of God's Word. God's Word is relevant for all aspects of school life. The Bible is the final authority in all areas of Christian education. The school must embrace the idea that all truth is God's truth. [33]

Therefore when hiring staff for a school it is important for the administrator to ask questions to determine the candidate's worldview. The staff you hire must have a vibrant walk with the Lord Jesus Christ. The candidate must be actively involved in a local Bible teaching church. Look for candidates who have a vibrant walk with Christ, a passion for teaching, and competence in their field.

Be sure to include questions to determine the candidate's Christian walk on the application form. Two sample application forms are included at the end of this chapter. These may be helpful as you design your own forms.

Position Descriptions

It is important to write position descriptions for each staff position including teachers, janitorial staff, administrative staff, and any other type of position at your school. Position descriptions outline what an individual is to do as a part of the school organization. They define a particular piece of the school's mission, objectives, and action plans in which an individual will participate, and how one is to perform. The position description is the practical link between the planning process and the implementation of those plans, and it is the most effective means of communicating specific expectations and responsibilities from the school to the individual. It is a guiding document for the individual, whether administrator, secretary, teacher, janitor, or even volunteer, and therefore it must be clear, detailed, and complete.

Although there may be natural resistance to the perceived restrictions that position descriptions appear to present, it is this very setting of boundaries for an employee's work that organizes the work so assigned tasks can be accomplished in an effective and efficient way. Position descriptions are people oriented and serve to structure a person's daily tasks—something most people welcome.

Position descriptions will aid in many ways. They can:
- Define the responsibilities of a position. This definition sets the boundaries and structure of a specific position as it relates to all other jobs in the school. Position

responsibilities serve as a basis for establishing specific performance objectives on which the school and staff member can agree.

- Provide a criterion for recruiting, interviewing, and selection. Details about a job and its responsibilities will help define what a position entails and thus this will naturally make recruiting, interviewing, and selection of a new employee easier.

- Maximize understanding about the duties and responsibilities of a position. With a set listing of duties, an individual and supervisor can better communicate about what is required.

- Help a school know if there is proper delegation of duties. By comparing the listed duties of various positions work can be delegated to the level where it can best be performed. This review will also help an organization determine if all essential functions are assigned or if duplication of effort exists.

- Serve as a basis for meaningful performance evaluations. Both the supervisor and staff member have a better opportunity for an evaluation oriented to objectives when specific responsibilities are outlined and understood. A periodic self-evaluation is also possible with established goals, so there are no surprises when the formal evaluation is received.

- Act as a training aid. Position descriptions can help identify areas where training is needed, if individuals are not able to perform certain work requirements. Training can then be directed toward these areas.

- Provide objective criteria for corrective action, reprimand, or termination. With written duties and requirements, there should be fewer questions about whether disciplinary action

is justified when the work is not performed up to standards
(after training has been provided).

- Show compliance with equal employment opportunity
  requirements. Statements in position descriptions that
  clearly define job requirements may serve as evidence
  against possible charges of discrimination under equal
  employment opportunity rules.
- Serve as a basis for setting wage and salary grades. Especially
  in a large school, position descriptions are essential when
  setting wage and salary levels, so comparisons of duties and
  responsibilities can be made objectively.

Position descriptions arise from a need to define what people
are to do and how they are to perform effectively in an organization,
within the context of the entire organization's objectives. With
this broad goal in mind, a position description must be prepared
carefully, and the necessary time taken to make it a document
that will not only define what is to be done, but also motivate an
individual effectively.

When writing position descriptions include the following:

1. A short statement describing the position and general
   responsibilities, followed by a listing of more specific
   responsibilities. These should be clear and as detailed
   as possible, generally in descending order of importance.
   However, remember that these are "responsibility"
   statements, not detailed procedural statements. For
   example, the responsibility of an administrative assistant
   may be to "order supplies as needed." How supplies are to be
   ordered would appear in an office procedure guide.
2. An individual's line of accountability should be included.
   This section also may include important points of
   coordination within other positions.

3. The skills required for the position should be listed, some in detail if they pertain to technical abilities. For example, there can be a big difference between "know how to use a computer," and "be proficient in the following computer programs: Excel, Access…"

4. Required education and experience should be shown, including the type of education and amount and type of experience required.

5. Special requirements or working conditions should be discussed if these are pertinent to the job needs. There may be special licenses required or unusual duty hours that need to be listed.

6. The final responsibility statement should be quite general to allow inclusion of "other responsibilities and tasks that may be requested from time to time."

Remember that a position description names the factors and requirements of the work to be done, not a person who may fill the position. Also remember that, to be a positive, motivating document, the position description should be carefully reviewed with new staff members or volunteers, who should be provided a copy. The date the position description was prepared or last revised should be recorded on the document.

There are several considerations to make when writing position descriptions:

-   Always write or revise a position description for a new position before recruiting and interviewing begins. The position description should serve as the major criterion by which candidates are judged during the interviewing and selection process.

-   Always review and rewrite a position description for an

existing position that has been vacated and for which a replacement is planned. This is the best time to make changes in position responsibilities, if needed.

- In situations in which position descriptions do not currently exist, introduce the development process carefully. People may view the change as a restriction on their freedom or perhaps even as a way to define them out of a job, rather than as a means to set positive parameters for performance.

- Involve the staff in defining work performance requirements. Try to make it a team effort, something in which all are involved and have ownership, rather than a directive from management. Incumbents can participate by describing their own work requirements, being careful not to describe themselves. For open positions, supervisors may want to draft the initial description and have staff members with whom the person filling the open position will interact, review and comment on the draft.

- Use a standard format so different positions can be seen in relationship to each other.

- Be sure to build in occasions for periodic review and updates. Position descriptions can easily become outdated as requirements change and should be reviewed at least every two years.

- Finally, management should review all position descriptions to ensure that, as a group, they adequately describe what needs to be done to meet organizational goals and objectives.

The position description becomes the guide to develop specific, measurable, time-related goals and objectives for each individual. Generally, one or more specific objectives can be developed for most of the responsibility statements in a position description.

At the end of this chapter is a sample work sheet for developing position descriptions and there is also a sample position description for a teacher in a Christian school. Remember, however, that each position description must be customized to the circumstances and uniqueness of each position.

Interviewing To Fill A Position

The interview is perhaps the most important time you will spend with an applicant. The decision to hire can lead to a long-term, productive, and mutually satisfying relationship—or just the opposite.

An interview is your opportunity to get to know a candidate and to determine whether he can meet the requirements of the open position. The candidate will have questions although you should expect that he will have done his homework and be somewhat familiar with the organization and the position for which he is applying. Together, you will each be trying to determine whether there will be a proper "fit" of the candidate with the existing organization and the supporting environment. A positive interview should be one in which both the organization and the interviewee find out as much as possible about each other and know at the end of the interview whether the candidate is right for the open position.

Staff Training

After you have your staff in place you will need to provide training for the staff. This training must be ongoing. The Christian school teacher needs to be growing continually in his understanding of students and the issues that impact their lives. Such growth requires prayer, insight, and training. Training should include Biblical studies, perhaps taught by a local pastor or other qualified Bible teacher. There should also be training on the teaching-learning process that is so vital in order for teaching and learning to take place in the school. Teaching is helping people learn. The basic problem for the school is not teaching, but learning. Unless we understand how people learn, we won't be able to teach.

Almost all of the major Christian publishing companies that publish curriculum also offer a wide array of support material that includes a list of teaching methodologies and step-by-step procedures for implementing them in a variety of classroom contexts. Many publishing companies will also provide workshops to train the teachers who will be using their products.

Other training topics should include childhood development, classroom management/discipline, discipleship, curriculum issues, and the use of technology in the classroom. A training schedule should be maintained and new staff members must agree to participate in the training program. A commitment to learning implies that teachers in Christian schools will continue to grow professionally. Failure to grow personally as a Christian educator diminishes one's ministry. To be satisfied with minimal preparedness devalues students and teachers alike.

The Christian teacher has the unique opportunity to mentor and disciple students and then enables them to grow in ways much deeper than would be possible in a typical government school classroom. Mentoring is a shepherding process. Because Christian teachers have a calling and a mission, it is imperative that they model Christ as they interact with their students. If we educate people intellectually but fail to touch their souls, we have not achieved our mission as Christian teachers.

Learning and cognitive growth are to be pursued vigorously, but with a difference. In the Christian school, the purpose for academic pursuits is not personal gain; rather, the focus is to advance the Kingdom of God. Knowledge is valuable when used to follow God's Will. Excellence in Christian education implies that all students are challenged to develop their gifts from God. How teachers view their role as educators greatly influences the way they teach.

The teachers must be skilled in training students in cognitive development. Cognitive development happens when the learners participate in higher level thinking processes. The ability to apply facts and to think critically and creatively is essential. Academic leadership implies that teachers plan and teach for cognitive growth.

Teachers committed to cognitive development are also committed to ongoing assessment, which provides information that directs future lesson structures and learning activities.

Teacher Evaluations

Teachers in Christian schools are strategically positioned to demonstrate competence, both academically and spiritually. The administrator of the school should evaluate teachers periodically. There should be a checklist of areas that will be evaluated and this checklist should be provided to the teachers at the beginning of the year. The teacher should provide a copy of the lesson plan for each subject for each week. During the evaluation the administrator should visit the classroom with a copy of the teacher's lesson plan, the position description, and the evaluation checklist. During the visit he should take notes of his observations. After the visit the administrator and the teacher should meet to discuss the evaluation. The lesson plans and evaluation forms should be kept in the teacher's personnel folder in the administrator's files.

The administrator should feel free to visit classrooms for informal visits as well. Of course the administrator should be careful not to disrupt the classroom with his visits. However, his presence in the classrooms and other places on the campus on a regular basis provides another role model for the students. Also, the administrator is less likely to distract the students during formal visits if they are accustomed to seeing him often in their classrooms and on the campus. The administrator's frequent visits to the classrooms will also give him a real sense of what is happening on the campus.

Sample Application form for Certified Staff
Name of School and Contact Information.
Employment Application (Certified)

Position Desired: _____

Application Date:_____Date Available: _____

Your interest in (Name of School) is appreciated. We realize that the key to a successful Christian school is its staff. We are grateful for those who are professionally qualified, who really love children, and who, by the pattern of their lives, exemplify Christ.

We look forward to receiving your application. Thank you for your interest in (Name of School) It is our prayer that God will fulfill His perfect will in the lives of all applicants.

A. NAME AND ADDRESS

Full Name:_____

Address: _____

_____

Phone: _____Best time to reach you:_____

B. PERSONAL INFORMATION

Marital Status Single _____ Engaged _____ Married _____ Separated _____

Spouse's name: _____Occupation: _____

Years Married: _____ # of children: _____

Ages: _____

C. POSITION DESIRED

( ) Administrator ( ) K ( )1-2 ( ) 3-4 ( ) 5-6 ( ) 7-8 ( ) Other:

Please list your preferences here: _____

Special Abilities/Sports/Clubs you would be willing and capable to direct:

_____

_____

D. CHRISTIAN BACKGROUND

* Please attach on a separate piece of paper and in your own handwriting your Christian testimony.

Bible: Do you believe the Bible to be the ONLY inspired and infallible Word of God, our final authority in all matters of faith, conduct, and truth?   (   ) Yes (   ) No

Signature: _____

Statement of Faith: Please read our Statement of Faith and indicate below your degree of support.

_____ I fully support the Statement as written without mental reservations.

Signature: _____

Church: Denomination/Church you attend:_____

Years attended: _____

Pastor's Name: _____Phone:_____

Service: In what church activities are you involved and with what degree of regularity?

_____

What other Christian service have you done since becoming a Christian? _____

_____

What is your attitude toward working with those of other races?

_____

_____

What is your attitude toward working with those of other denominational beliefs? _____

_____

_____

Are you capable of teaching a Bible class? Explain:

_____

_____

_____

Devotional Life: Describe your routine of personal Bible study and prayer:

_____

_____

What books have you read recently that have helped you spiritually?

_____

_____

E. PROFESSIONAL QUALIFICATIONS

* Please attach photocopies of all college transcripts. Official copies will be required should you be offered a position.

Formal Training: What degree(s) do you hold?

Degree	Date Received	Institution

_____

_____

_____

_____

_____

Your Major(s): _____

Your Minor(s): _____

Cumulative GPA for BA: _____ Graduate work: _____

Work Experience

List your education-related experience with the most recent first.

Location Grade/Subject/Position Dates

_____

_____

_____

_____

Total number of years teaching experience:

Public: _____ Christian _____

Reason for leaving your most recent position: _____

_____

_____

Other experience:

List other work or military experience that may have significance for the type of position

for which you are applying.

Place   Type of work/experience   Dates

_____

_____

_____

Teaching Credentials

Do you have a valid ACSI certificate? _____ Level: _____

Valid for: _____

Do you have a valid state teaching certificate? _____

State _____Expires _____

List any endorsements you have:

_____

_____

_____

Christian School Preparation

Have you ever had any courses in the Christian Philosophy of Education? If so, when and where? _____

_____

If not, would you be willing to take such a course by correspondence or otherwise? _____

_____

*Attach a typed copy of your personal Christian Philosophy of education

Have you ever been charged, arrested or convicted of a crime? If yes, explain._____

_____

_____

F. PERSONAL REFERENCES

Please sign the Reference Release Form that is attached and return it with this application. Do not list family members or relatives for references. Give three references who are qualified to speak concerning your professional training and experience. List your current or most recent principal or supervisor first.

Name	Complete Address	Phone	Position

Give three references who are qualified to speak concerning your spiritual experience and Christian service. List your current pastor first.

Name   Complete Address   Phone   Position

_____

_____

_____

_____

G. PERSONAL PHILOSOPHY

On a separate piece of paper, please briefly answer each question below.

1. Why do you wish to teach in a Christian school?
2. What are the main characteristics that distinguish a Christian school from a public school?
3. What do you consider to be the proper classroom atmosphere for learning?
4. What is your philosophy of discipline? What is your attitude toward corporal punishment?
5. What areas do you feel are your strengths? Weaknesses?

Please summarize any additional information that you would like to present regarding your candidacy for this position.

H. APPLICANT'S CERTIFICATION AND AGREEMENT

I understand that (Name of School) does not discriminate in its employment practices against any person because of race, color, national or ethnic origin, gender, or handicap. I further understand that any offer of employment is conditioned on the proof of legal authority to work in the U.S.

I hereby certify that the facts set forth in this application are true and complete to the best of my knowledge. I understand that discovery of falsification of any statement or significant omission of fact during any phase of the hiring process may prevent me from being hired or if hired may make me subject to immediate dismissal.

I authorize (Name of School) to perform a background check and to inquire about my work and personal history. I further authorize (Name of School) to verify all data given in my application for employment, related papers, and my oral interviews. I authorize the release and giving of any information requested by (Name of School) such as employment records, performance reviews, and personal references. I release any person, organization, or company from liability or damage which may result from furnishing the information requested. I further waive the right to ever personally view any references given by (Name of School).

I further certify that I have carefully read and do understand the above statements.

_____

Signature of Applicant   Date

Sample Application Form for Non-certified Staff
Name of School and Contact Information.
Employment Application (Non-Certified)

Your interest in (Name of School) is appreciated. We realize that the key to a successful Christian school is its staff. We are grateful for those who are professionally qualified, who really love children, and who, by the pattern of their lives, exemplify Christ. We look forward to receiving your application. Thank you for your interest in (Name of School). It is our prayer that God will fulfill His perfect will in the lives of all applicants.

A. NAME AND ADDRESS

Full Name:_____

Address: _____

_____

Phone: _____Best time to reach you:

B. PERSONAL INFORMATION

Marital Status Single _____ Engaged _____ Married _____ Separated _____

Spouse's name: _____Occupation: _____

Years Married: _____ # of children: _____

Ages: _____

C. POSITION DESIRED

( ) Administrator ( ) K ( )1-2 ( ) 3-4 ( ) 5-6 ( ) 7-8 ( ) Other:

Please list your preferences here: _____

Special Abilities/Sports/Clubs you would be willing and capable to direct: _____

_____

D. CHRISTIAN BACKGROUND

* Please attach on a separate piece of paper and in your own handwriting your Christian testimony.

Bible: Do you believe the Bible to be the ONLY inspired and infallible Word of God, our final authority in all matters of faith, conduct, and truth?   (   ) Yes (   ) No

Signature: _____

Statement of Faith

Statement of Faith: Please read our Statement of Faith and indicate below your degree of support.

_____ I fully support the Statement as written without mental reservations.

Signature: _____

Church: Denomination/Church you attend: _____

Years attended: _____

Pastor's Name: _____Phone: _____

Devotional Life: Describe your routine of personal Bible study and prayer:

_____

_____

E. PROFESSIONAL QUALIFICATIONS

Formal Training: What certificate(s), diploma(s), degree(s) do you hold?

Certificate/Diploma/Degree   Date Received
Institution

_____

_____

_____

_____

_____

Work Experience: List your work experience with the most recent first: Location   Position   Dates

_____

_____

_____   _____

_____

_____

F. PERSONAL REFERENCES

Please sign the Reference Release Form that is attached and return
it with this application. Do not list family members or relatives
for references. Give three references who are qualified to speak
concerning your professional training and experience. List your
current or most recent principal or supervisor first.

Name   Complete Address   Phone   Position

_____

_____

_____

_____

_____

Give three references who are qualified to speak concerning your
spiritual experience and Christian service. List your current pastor first.

Name   Complete Address   Phone   Position

_____

_____

_____

_____

Have you ever been charged, arrested or convicted of a crime? If
yes, explain

_____

_____

_____

_____

G. PERSONAL PHILOSOPHY

On a separate piece of paper, please briefly answer each question below.

1. Why do you wish to work in a Christian school?_____

2. What are the main characteristics that distinguish a Christian school from a public school?

3. What areas do you feel are your strengths? Weaknesses?

Please summarize any additional information that you would like to present regarding your candidacy for this position.

H. APPLICANT'S CERTIFICATION AND AGREEMENT

I understand that (Name of School) does not discriminate in its employment practices against any person because of race, color, national or ethnic origin, gender, or handicap. I further understand that any offer of employment is conditioned on the proof of legal authority to work in the U.S.

I hereby certify that the facts set forth in this application are true and complete to the best of my knowledge. I understand that discovery of falsification of any statement or significant omission of fact during any phase of the hiring process may prevent me from being hired or if hired may make me subject to immediate dismissal.

I authorize (Name of School) to perform a background check and to inquire about my work and personal history. I further authorize (Name of School) to verify all data given in my application for employment, related papers, and my oral interviews. I authorize the release and giving of any information requested by (Name of School) such as employment records, performance reviews, and personal references. I release any person, organization, or company from liability or damage which may result from furnishing the information requested. I further waive the right to ever personally view any references given by (Name of School)

I further certify that I have carefully read and do understand the above statements.

_____

Signature of Applicant   Date

Position Description Work Sheet

Position: _____

General Responsibility Statement:_____
_____
_____

Specific Responsibilities:

1. _____
2. _____
3. _____
4. _____
5. _____
6. _____
7. _____
8. _____
9. _____

Qualifications, Education, Experience required for this position:

_____
_____
_____
_____
_____

Revision date:_____

Example Position Description for
a Christian School Teacher

Position: Christian School Teacher
General Responsibility Statement: To prayerfully help students learn subject matter, skills, and attitudes that will contribute to their development as mature, able, and responsible Christian men and women to the praise and glory of God

Responsibilities:

Spiritual
1. Seeks to role-model in speech, actions, and attitudes, a consistent walk with Jesus Christ.
2. Shows by example the importance of prayer, Scripture memorization and study, witnessing, and unity in Christian fellowship.
3. Follows the Matthew 18 principle in dealing with students, administration, and staff.
4. Motivates students to accept God's gift of salvation and grow in their faith.
5. Leads students to a realization of their self-worth in Christ.
6. Encourages and directs in Christian service activity.

Instructional
1. Recognizes the role of parents as primarily responsible before God for their child's education and assists them in the task.
2. Teaches classes as assigned following prescribed scope and sequence as scheduled by the principal.
3. Plans broadly through the use of the semester and quarterly plans and objectives, and more currently through the use of the lesson plan book.
4. Integrates Biblical principles and the Christian philosophy of education throughout the curriculum.
5. Effects student learning through mastery of the subject material by utilizing valid teaching techniques to achieve curriculum goals within the framework of the school's philosophy.
6. Plans a program of study that, as much as possible, meets the individual

needs, interests, and abilities of the students, challenging each to do his best work.

7. Employs a variety of instructional aids, methods and materials that will provide for creative teaching to reach the whole child: spiritual, mental, physical, social, and emotional.

8. Plans through approved channels the balanced use of field trips, guest lectures, and other media.

9. Uses homework effectively for drill, review, enrichment or project work.

10. Assesses the learning of students on a regular basis and provides progress reports as required.

11. Keeps proper discipline in the classroom and on the school premises for a good teaching environment.

12. Informs the administration if unable to fulfill any duty assigned. Prepares adequate information and materials for a substitute teacher.

13. Maintains a punctual attitude in the classroom and expects classes to begin promptly.

Non-Instructional

1. Cooperates with the Board and administration in implementing all policies, procedures, and directives governing the operation of the school.

2. Maintains regular and accurate attendance and grade records to meet the demands for a comprehensive knowledge of each student's progress.

3. Keeps students, parents, and the administration adequately informed of progress or deficiencies and gives sufficient notice of failure.

4. Maintains a clean, attractive, well-ordered classroom, with attention to bulletin boards, chalk boards, book storage, and furniture arrangement.

5. Supervises extra-curricular activities, organizations, and outings as assigned.

6. Supports the broader programs of the school by attending extracurricular activities when possible.

Professional

1. Utilizes educational opportunities and evaluation processes for professional growth.
2. Seeks the counsel of the principal, colleagues, and parents while maintaining a teachable attitude.
3. Provides input and recommendations for administrative and managerial functions in the school.
4. Attends and participates in scheduled devotional, inservice, retreat, committee, faculty, and P.T.F. meetings.
5. Knows the procedures for dealing with issues of an emergency nature.
6. Contributes to the general improvement of the school program.
7. Refuses to use or circulate confidential information inappropriately.
8. Performs any other duties that may be assigned by the administration.

Personal

1. Demonstrates the character qualities of enthusiasm, courtesy, flexibility, integrity, gratitude, kindness, self-control, perseverance, and punctuality.
2. Meets everyday stress with emotional stability, objectivity, and optimism.
3. Develops and maintains rapport with students, parents, and staff by treating others with friendliness, dignity, and consideration.
4. Respectfully submits and is loyal to constituted authority.
5. Maintains a personal appearance that is a role model of cleanliness, modesty, good taste, and in agreement with school policy.
6. Uses acceptable English in written and oral communication. Speaks with clear articulation.
7. Recognizes the need for good public relations. Represents the school in a favorable and professional manner to the constituency and general public.
8. Places the teaching ministry ahead of outside or volunteer work.
9. Makes an effort to appreciate and understand the uniqueness of the community.

Evaluation: Performance of these responsibilities will be evaluated in accordance with provisions of the Board's policy on Evaluation of Professional Personnel.

Qualifications: The teacher shall be one who has received Jesus Christ as Savior and Lord. The teacher shall be a member in good standing of an evangelical Bible teaching church, He/she shall be a person of spiritual maturity with academic and leadership abilities. The teacher shall reflect the purpose of the school which is to honor Christ in every class and in every activity. The teacher shall be one who feels called of God to the teaching position being sought. Other qualifications may be added by the Board as deemed appropriate.

Contracted By: (Name of School) School Board upon recommendation of the principal for one year.

Responsible To: Principal/(Name of School)

Supervises: Volunteers and student aides working in his/her classroom.

Revision date: November 21, 2011

Chapter Five:
The School's Expectations for the Students and the Student Code of Conduct

Proverbs 1:7 "The fear of the Lord is the beginning of knowledge, but fools despise wisdom and discipline." [34]

A Christian school must set high standards for the students who will be attending the school. There should be high expectations for the students' academic success, behavior, and deportment. Students should be expected to treat others with respect. They should be living a Christian life.

The school should produce a Parent/Student Handbook. The handbook should include contact information, the overall philosophy of the school, vision, mission, statement of faith, Christian philosophy of education, admissions policy and procedure, information about tuition, scholarships, attendance policy, the school schedule, information about the curriculum and staff, safety procedures, grading policy, dress code, curriculum, and the school's discipline policy and code. You should also include an agreement form for the parents and students to sign. If you are a new school starting out you may want to ask other Christian schools for a copy of their student/parent handbook. These will serve as examples and help you to develop your own handbook and code of conduct.

The handbook will serve as a tool to help familiarize the parents and students with your school, the staff, the curriculum, and specific school policies. The guidelines provided should be established with the student's and the school's best interest in mind. It should show what your school offers and what your school expects from the students and parents.

In developing the school's handbook remember that your mission is to prayerfully come alongside familes to instruct, encourage, and inspire students to become truth-seeking Christ-like individuals and godly leaders.

Dress Code

Consider if you want to have a school uniform. There are many advantages to requiring students to wear uniforms to school. Uniforms instill an appreciation for the corporate community of the school and can also be effective in addressing peer-pressure that can arise regarding who has the "latest fashion". A uniform doesn't have to be expensive. It can be as simple as a white polo shirt and navy blue skirts or pants (or any color combination the school chooses). The school may have some shirts made with the school logo on it.

A committee including parents, teachers, and administrators may be formed to decide on a school dress code. A typical dress code is included to help you get started.

Sample Dress Code
Boys School Clothing

- Pants/Shorts: khaki, navy, or black, all of which must be worn with a belt if there are belt loops.
- Shirts: long or short sleeved, with a collar, solid color shirts, all of which must be tucked in.
- Shoes: tennis, dress, or sandals with a closed back. No flip-flops or clogs.

Girls School Clothing
- Pants/Shorts: khaki, navy, or black, all of which must be worn with a belt if there are belt loops. No leggings.
- Skirts, skorts, or jumpers: khaki, navy, or black, must be to knees.
- Shirts: long or short sleeved, with a collar, solid color shirts, all of which must be tucked in.
- Shoes: tennis, dress, or sandals with a closed back. no flip-flops or clogs.

Clarifications
- All skirts, jumpers, and skorts, must be to the knees when sitting.
- All pants, skirts, jumpers, shirts, blouses, or skorts must be a solid color. This excludes stripes, flowers, decoraive patches, insignias, etc. Only the school logo is acceptable.
- Hair should be clean, neat and an appropriate length.
- Students are expected to appear neat, and clean during the school day.
- Girls may wear one pair of simple earrings, no dangles or larger than a dime and no other piercings. Boys may not wear earrngs or other piercings.
- If a child arrives at school inappropriately dressed, the parent will be asked to bring him/her a change of clothes.

Discipline Code
There should also be a committee comprised of the administrator, teachers, and parents to develop the school's discipline code. The committee should borrow student handbooks from other Christian schools to get ideas. It is not necessary to reinvent the wheel, but the committee shouldn't just copy another

school's discipline code without a discussion to see what specifically is needed for their school. Keep in mind when writing a discipline code that you are seeking to provide an environment where the students are encouraged and challenged to exemplify Christian behavior in all aspects of the school day. One purpose of discipline is to maintain the peace and excellent learning atmosphere of the school. Another purpose is maintaining the safey of the students. It is imperative that the school be a haven of safety for all children. Actions that jeopardize the safety of others should be dealt with promptly and according to the school policies. A third purpose of discipline is instruction in godliness. Studnets learn and grow in the Lord when disciplined appropriately, by using God's means, for God's glory and honor.

Firm discipline, administered with compassion and understading is an absolute Biblical mandate for child training. Remember that you are to work with the family and home, not take the place of the parents. Support the parental enforcement as guided in Proverbs 23:13. "Do not withhold discipline from a child. If you punish him with the rod, he will not die." [35]

Discipline is an act of love when applied consistently. It separates a child from an inappropriate attitude or action which would otherwise be destructive to him or others. Proper discipline is never administered in anger. When a student misbehaves, a consequence corresponding to the severity of the offence is assigned to him. Consequences together with reproof (explaining why the action was wrong and what would be correct according to biblical references) are designed to bring repentance and a decision in the child to do what is right in the future.

Some typical disciplinary consequences used by Christian

schools include the following:

1.) Parent/Teacher/Student conferences.
2.) Student separated from the rest of the class for a period of time.
3.) Student required to stay in during recess or at break time.
4.) Detention—A child is detained for a specified amount of time and assigned to do a task which is in correlation to the offense. Detention is the most frequently used consequence for minor offenses. Detention could be served after school with one day's notice to the parents.
5.) Suspension—A student is suspended when his behavior or attitudes are such that he should be temporarily removed from fellowship with his peers. This protects other students and gives the offender time to reconsider his position. Students on suspension receive unexcused absences for days absent and will thus receive zeros for all work missed.
6.) Expulsion—this is isused as a last resort for a student who is severely or habitually misbehaving. This consequence is a permanent removal from the school.

Good discipline means that the classroom is relatively free from confusion, disorder, and anti-social behavior. It means that each child and the group as a whole operate freely within a structured framework which they understand, accept, and incorporate into their behavior without constant reminders. Effective discipline develops a maximum of self-direction, and a sense of responsibility. It helps a child to know and accept himself. Effective discipline is based on justice and equal opportunity. It should help a child to change his perception of a situation. Effective discipline must be consistent. Effective discipline is essential in a classroom in order for learning to take place.

Discipline is something that needs to be learned. Acceptable behavior in a classroom and on the playground with a group of students needs to be taught as one would teach any other subject. Some of the following suggestions may prove helpful in developing positive discipline.

1. Children need to be given standards to follow in their conduct, and opportunities to practice acceptable conduct.
2. Children are ready for different types of learning at varioius stages of development. The administrator must be familiar with the general characteristices of each developmental age.
3. Children learn best when their trust and affection makes them want to please the person in authority.
4. Children differ in their needs and responses.
5. No method of discipline is equally effective with all children. A few stern words may stop the giggles of one child but may make another giggle more.
6. Children do not learn good behavior chiefly by being punished for their misdeeds. They learn by example, instruction, practice, and their mistakes.
7. It is important that everyone develop the ability to forgive and forget.

Sometimes a school will make a classification system of offenses. Here is an example of a classification system made by one school. [36]

Class A
DISTURBANCE: 1st offense student conference with staff

Being in unauthorized areas

Tardiness (more than 3 times)

Violation of class rules

Playing, running, making noise in a quiet area

Littering

Dress code infraction

Hurtful teasing

Rough-housing

Violation of playground rules

Class B
HAZARDS AND VERBAL ABUSE: 1st offense conference: parent & student

Repetitive teasing

Open disrespect to staff

Hitting, shoving, rock throwing

Abuse of school property

Foul language/profanity including sexual or crude-vulgarity

Failure to cooperate/obey at any time

Taking property without permission

Class C
MORAL OFFENSE (2nd degree): 1st offense suspesion

Explcit refusal to obey

Verbal abuse to staff

Cutting class

Lying

Cheating

Stealing

Forgery

Gambilng

Use of or possession of tobacco products

Fighting

Minor vandalism

Class D
MORAL OFFENSES (1st degree): 1st offense is expulsion
  Sexual immorality
  Assaulting a staff member
  Possession or sale of pornographic material
  Weapons
  Use, possession or sale of alcohol or drugs on campus
  Drunkenness on/off campus
  Serious vandalism

The administrator should develop procedures for dealing with discipline in the school and discuss the procedures with the entire staff. A typical procedure is included here for your convenience.

Sample Procedure for Discipline [37]
Except for minor classroom violations, the following will take place when a staff memeber discovers that a student has committed an offense.
1.   The student will be informed of his offense by means of a conference with staff.
2.   A staff member will write out a citation form describing the offense.
3.   The citation form will be recorded by the student's teacher, sent home for parents to see, and should be returned signed by the parents to indicate that the parents have been notified.
4.   In a discplianry suspension or expulsion case a conference will be held with the student, parents, teacher, and administrator.

Remember the purpose of the discipline code is to maintain a Christian environment that is condusive to learning and where everyone is safe.

Take some time to study the student handbooks of several Christian schools to gain insight and to get ideas for making your own handbook.

Remember a well ordered school where everyone is respectful is essential to produce an environment where learning can take place. Hold your students to high expectations and they will succeed.

Chapter Six:
Physical Property:
Buildings, Equipment and Other Facilities

Ephesians 4:1 "As a prisoner for the Lord, then, I urge you to live a life worthy of the calling you have received." [38]

It is important that the physical plant of the school have a professional appearance and an atmosphere that is welcoming and conducive to learning in a Christian environment. It must be clean, in good repair and well organized. When the school is just getting started it may seek to share the facilities with a church even if it is an independent school. After the school grows the board can research the possibility to acquiring its own property. In addition to real property the school will also have equipment and furniture and other items that will need to be maintained and the school has the responsibility to maintain records on all of the property it owns. A record book should be made of all property and inventory should be made on a regular schedule. The record book can be computerized, but a hard copy should be printed periodically and the computer record must be backed up to a disk from time to time. For each piece of equipment you should include an identification number, the name of the item, purchase date (if purchased as a used item use the manufacture date), place of purchase, model number and serial number, warranty information, location of item, and a record of maintenance and repairs for the item.

The proper management of school property will consume a significant amount of time and resources. In addition to facility planning and maintenance organization and staffing, there are several important review procedures which should be followed in order to properly maintain the school property:

- Responsibilities for maintenance, current and preventive, must be clear.
- Regular maintenance schedules must be established and kept.
- Periodic inspection of facilities must be completed.
- Replacement planning and programs must be active.
- Property and insurance inventory records need to be complete.

Who takes care of this important area? Most schools have specific groups responsible for property maintenance, such as the trustees or a property committee. In a small school this might be the administrator's responsibility. The ultimate responsibility will rest with these groups, and they must be proactive in their approach. Their part of the total mission of the school must be understood and specific action plans prepared. They must be fully supported by the staff and school board as well as recognized periodically for their contribution to the life of the school. An active preventive maintenance program and involvement of staff and school families in "work days" or a "weekly maintenance party" of volunteers will help to cement the understanding of the school families and staff about this important area.

If the school has a custodian, this individual usually becomes the primary contact point for all custodial duties and minor repairs. The work of the custodian must be organized by schedules and checklists. The custodian must know when to inspect facilities and equipment and how to correct concerns. This individual must also be familiar with equipment and how it works, as well as with tools and how to use and store them. The staff members must be encouraged to respect the work schedule of the custodian and refrain from requesting special work that has not been scheduled. To help with this the school secretary or administrator should have a form available for teachers to fill out if they have any maintenance needs for their classrooms. These completed forms should be approved by the administrator before being distributed to the custodian.

In a small school, there may not be a custodian. In some small schools the administrator actually takes on the tasks of the custodian. He may involve parent volunteers or others in the day-to-day custodial duties. In this context it is even more important to stress schedules, who is in charge, when things will be done, and what funds are or are not available for needed maintenance. A schedule of maintenance needs should be developed, posted, and items checked off as they are completed. Often the staff and school families are involved in work projects. They become fully supportive of the custodial efforts.

Because regular inspection to recognize problems and correct them is so important to any school, someone needs to ensure that maintenance has been done well, that items needing repair have been identified, that checklists are current and posted, and that there is follow-up on maintenance concerns.

Who inspects and follows up? In larger schools, a business manager may fill this need. Or, trustees or a property committee member may be responsible. In most schools, the custodian, the school administrator, or a designated board member may perform these reviews.

Once a need is identified the problem must be communicated to someone who is responsible for either fixing it or scheduling it to be done. One needs to be specific about who will do the work and, how, and when it will be done. A simple, standard form can be used to record the problem, solution, when fixed, and a date for follow-up.

When major repairs are necessary, the trustees or property committee must take the lead, whether in a large or small school. There should always be a thorough assessment of the need to repair or replace an item.

Rules for equipment use should be established and posted. Staff and volunteers should be encouraged to learn how to use equipment, activate utilities, clean up their areas, and so forth. They must know who can provide help and training. If no custodian is on duty, every staff member and every volunteer must assume they are individually responsible for maintenance and security.

The school administrator constantly needs to remind the staff, students, and volunteers to respect the need for good property use and maintenance. Staff members working after hours need to be reminded to turn off the lights and lock up. Repair needs should be monitored and communicated positively to the custodian or property committee for action. Staff and volunteers need to know where to pick up a maintenance request form to report problems.

This important area needs to be organized. Anticipate and prepare for major problems and replacement. Encourage participation by all, but have responsibility clearly set. The items which follow will assist you with this process.

Standards, Guidelines, and Checklists

Written standards and guidelines describing jobs, maintenance schedules, and disaster preparedness are invaluable. Proper use of school property and a consideration for the safety of the students and staff requires a certain amount of paperwork and some active organization.

A bulletin board might be provided in the custodial area for posting lists and schedules. It can also post names and telephone numbers of people to contact in case of problems. Specific guidelines might include:

- Inspection checklists
- Cleaning schedules (especially seasonal requirements)
- Painting schedules
- Repair procedures
- Procedure to follow when problems arise

Custodial checklists include such things as what needs to be cleaned and when; which tools to use; and which items to observe and check while cleaning. Detailed operating instructions for major equipment should to be posted near the place where the equipment is stored. Schedules for use of facilities need to be posted in a common area.

Guidelines for volunteer help should be available at the place where tools and equipment are kept and should include:

- Procedures for equipment use
- Clear instructions for the proper tools to use for a given job
- Times or schedules for doing certain tasks
- Checklists for inspections
- Instructions for operating tools and equipment

Guidelines may be posted in individual rooms and include:

- What to do when entering the property, such as how to turn on the air conditioning, how to turn on the amplification system, how to use any special equipment that is located in that room, and so forth.
- What to do to secure the property when leaving, such as what doors to check, windows to close, electrical items to turn off, and so forth
- Procedures to follow in case of disasters

It is always best to overuse checklists and procedural statements. Equipment and facilities will be better used, maintained, and secured, and people kept safe.

Contingency Plans for Potential Disasters

Procedures and guidelines for handling potential disasters could be some of the most important documents ever prepared by a school. When a school opens its doors to the public, it assumes the legal, ethical, and moral responsibility for the safety and physical well being of those who enter those doors. Schools and their recreational facilities and various activities are prime targets for lawsuits, especially if there is no evidence of carefully prepared up-to-date contingency plans.

Depending on local need, contingency plans should exist for fire-related disasters; bomb threats; natural disasters including severe freezing weather, earthquakes, flooding, hurricanes, and tornadoes; power failures and interruption in telephone and utility services; and intruders or robbery. After plans are developed, they should be rehearsed, at least by the persons primarily involved in student safety and facility maintenance and security.

school secretary or administrator. Everyone should be encouraged
to remain calm and not panic, and the person in charge must do
everything possible to ensure this calm. If a bomb threat comes
in, one should get as much information as possible from the caller.
The evacuation should include room-by-room checks for persons
who may have been left behind. Give special consideration and
assistance to physically challenged persons and the younger students.
The school administrator should be the last person to leave the
building.

Natural Disasters

The contingency plan must include applicable procedures
and assigned responsibilities for each of the following scenarios
depending upon location:

Severe Freezing Weather:

a.   Keep a small amount of water running from the faucets of all
     sinks to prevent the pipes from freezing.
b.   Keep sidewalks clear and free of ice.
c.   Use ice-melting compounds if necessary.

Earthquakes:

a.   Turn off open-flame gas appliances.
b.   Keep everyone away from windows and appliances or
     supplies that may slide or topple over.
c.   Help people get to a doorway or under a table.
d.   Move to an open area if outside.
e.   Keep everyone away from buildings, walls, power lines, and
      power poles.
f.   After a severe earthquake, evacuate the building, check for
     fires and structural damage. Shut off utility supplies.

Flooding:

- When a flood warning is received, prepare the facility to lessen the possible damage.
- Store drinking water in closed sanitized containers normally used for food storage.
- Move everything off of the floor and low shelves.
- Secure all monies in a safe.
- Shut off the gas and electricity at the mains. If expected that electricity will be out for more than eight hours, move all perishables to another location.
- Do not reenter a flooded building until authorities have made a structural assessment.

Hurricanes:

a. Place masking tape on the windows from corner to corner making an "X" or if possible board up all windows. (If you live in an area where hurricanes are a frequent occurrence you should have special boards marked and available for quick installation when under a hurricane warning.)

b. Draw drapes or lower and close blinds to protect against flying glass.

c. Secure anything on the roof that may be loose.

d. Secure dumpster doors with rope.

e. Put trash containers and all moveable furniture, toys, and so forth indoors.

f. Notify the news media that all classes are canceled and that the school will be closed.

g. Everyone should remain indoors during a hurricane.

h. Follow all instructions issued by the local authorities.

Power Failures and Utility Interruption:

The contingency plans must address each of the following points, as they apply to the school or school related activity:

- Power Failure:
  a. Turn off gas appliances.
  b. Turn off equipment that uses a lot of power, such as exhaust hoods, warming lights, fryers, grills, computers, air conditioners, and so forth.
  c. If your facility is equipped with a generator, it should be started.
  d. When power is restored, turn one piece of equipment on at a time to prevent damage from a power surge.
  e. Keep refrigerators and freezers closed to maintain a safe food temperature for a longer period of time.

Telephone Service Interruption:

Find out if the outage is in your building or throughout the area. If service is available nearby, report the problem and arrange to use a nearby telephone or mobile phone in case of an emergency.

Be sure that someone is available to go for help if no telephone service is available.

- Interruption of Water Service:
  a. Do not allow use of the rest rooms as use can pose a serious health risk.
  b. If warned of an interruption in water service, fill as many clean containers as possible with water, wash all dirty dishes, and turn off the ice machine at the breaker panel to prevent damage.
- Gas Leak:
  a. If there is a gas smell, check pilots and related valves.

      b. If the smell persists, shut off the gas at the main and extinguish all open flames.

      c. Call the gas company.

Intrusion

An intrusion, especially by an armed person, can be an extremely tense and dangerous time. Special codes should be set up to alert everyone of an intrusion and the classroom teachers should lock the doors, cover the door windows, and have the students be silent and move to a safe corner of the room out of site. Procedure should dictate:

- During the intrusion:
  a. Stay calm.
  b. Be cooperative. Answer any questions promptly, but do not volunteer any information. Follow the perpetrator's directions.
  c. If possible signal someone to call the police without the perpetrator noticing.
  d. Observe and mentally note any physical characteristics, but do not be obvious about it.
  e. If able, notice the direction the perpetrator takes when leaving. If possible, try to see the type and color of the vehicle and the license number.
- Behavior to avoid:
  a. Never try to be a hero.
  b. Do not make sudden moves that may startle the perpetrator.
  c. Try not to panic.
  d. Avoid staring at the perpetrator, which may cause them to be nervous or hostile.

- Actions to take after the intrusion:
  a. Be ready to provide police with location, address, number of perpetrators involved, vehicle description, and so forth.
  b. Avoid discussing the incident until authorities arrive, so that all happenings are not distorted.
  c. Do not allow anyone to enter the area, so physical evidence is undisturbed.
- When the authorities arrive:
  a. Cooperate fully. Be certain when answering questions to give only the facts.
  b. If perpetrators are still present when authorities arrive, remain calm. Continue to cooperate with perpetrators and stay away from windows. Avoid calling attention to the fact that the authorities have arrived.
  c. Use good judgment.

Effective and Economical Insurance

Insurance on school property and services is essential, considering the liability risks for the school employees and in unforeseen accidents, as well as for protection against losses from fire, theft, and natural disasters.

Although it needs to be comprehensive, school insurance can also be economical. The first step is to define the risks, and then manage them for better, more economical coverage. Obviously, the goal of any school is survival in the face of a catastrophic loss. But after basic survival has been addressed, the school will want to lessen accidental loss through a risk assessment program, which in turn may lower insurance costs.

When dealing with loss exposure, a school should first look for ways to reduce or eliminate risk. For example, are there playground items that can be replaced with safer more modern equipment? Are there fire extinguishers, sprinkler systems, self-closing doors, handrails, and so forth, all of which enhance safety? Is there a regular program of maintenance inspection to ensure an optimum housekeeping program—and is something done about the problems found? Develop a checklist to use so that you will have a systematic way of identifying exposure and the chance for loss through self-inspection. Ask your insurance company, the local fire department and other local agencies for assistance in developing such a list. Then use the list to perform at least an annual review, with specific responsibility for the review clearly established.

A school intentionally may wish to accept some of the risk itself. A school may take on far more risk since most losses are partial losses. A higher deductible is an effective and normally economical way of accepting greater risk through some self-insurance. A school also should be clear on the value of its property, keeping some sort of inventory of property and furnishings. Many computers now come equipped with inventory programs suitable for a school. Videotaping the school and its contents is another excellent method of documentation. Don't forget to store the inventory and video in a safe place, preferably a safe-deposit box, or in another building.

The primary point of any active risk assessment program is that it allows for an organized approach to ascertaining what insurance coverage is needed, which then allows for purchasing only what is needed. Every school will differ; however, a risk assessment program will aid in identifying significant needs and differences.

When ready to purchase insurance, a school will want to carefully select an agent and company. One should examine whether the agency is knowledgeable about the school's unique needs and whether it insures a number of Christian schools. Is the agency willing to cover all phases of risk, such as workers' compensation and professional liability? Sometimes a school will find insurance agencies willing to write basic fire, theft, and liability coverage, but not interested or able to offer the unique coverage needed. Of course, claims responsiveness and billing procedures also may be important factors to consider.

The best coverage may be through group plans especially prepared for Christian schools. Substantial savings and greater coverage is often possible. These associations specialize in Christian school coverage and may be able to isolate unique risks.

In summary, every school should review its risk, establish responsibility for risk assessment, use a loss prevention checklist, choose an insurance program and agent carefully, keep an up-to-date inventory of property, and carry enough insurance to cover acceptable risk at an optimum price.

Chapter Seven:
Business Practices and Office Administration

Proverbs 24:3-4 "By wisdom a house is built, and through understanding it is established; through knowledge its rooms are filled with rare and beautiful treasures." [39]

This chapter will cover the areas of:
Office Administration
>   Public Relations/Marketing
>   Financial Practices
>   Professional Ethics

Office Administration

The primary administrative concern of the school administrator should be that vital resources available to the school are used effectively to achieve mission objectives. Those resources commonly include three things: human resources, school money, and school property. People are the greatest resource a school has. Nothing else matters or functions unless dedicated and committed people are involved. Both staff members and volunteers must be carefully chosen for work that fits them. They must be given adequate guidance about the tasks they are asked to do, through complete and clear position descriptions, policies, and procedures. Then they must be led, using the leadership style of a servant leader, one that is participatory and one that allows and expects a person to succeed. Progress toward more effective use of people's talents is possible only if we take time to assess, evaluate, and communicate with them about how they have met agreed-upon goals. See chapter four of this manual for more information about managing staff and volunteers.

The money that comes into the school must be used wisely in support of the school mission. It is very important to plan an annual budget that must be approved by the board. Accurate and timely reports showing what has been received for what purpose, and how it was used, are very important. Equally important is the process for handling and accounting for money as it is received. Donors like to know that their contributions are received and used for the purpose they intended. Almost nothing can undermine the mission of the school and its programs faster than questions about the credibility of its financial system. Administrators must be very sensitive to this and have enough knowledge about good financial control and accounting principles to recognize when the school may be in trouble, and then know when and how to seek help and make changes.

School property must be carefully and realistically planned for and acquired to fit the mission of the school. Planning should include long-range goals for improvement as well as general operating needs year by year. See chapter six of this manual for more information on property management.

When starting a new school one of the first things that should be done is to develop a mission statement. Make it a brief, succinct statement that tells all who read it why the school exists and what it strives to accomplish. A mission statement tends to be broad in scope and articulates a large vision. It generally does not refer to specific goals or objectives.

When the mission statement has been developed, discuss it with the entire staff and then publish it. Post it on bulletin boards and print it periodically in staff memos. It should be on the first page of the staff and student manuals.

From the mission statement a list of goals can be developed. Goals are statements of desired outcomes that support and expand upon various parts of the mission statement. Goals are more action oriented and establish the framework for specific actions and measurable objectives. Goals provide a specific direction for the work to be done in the school.

Another important task of office administration is record keeping. The administrator and his assistant/office secretary must develop an effective filing system that will make it easy to retrieve files when needed. There are several types of records that are necessary to keep in a school. A school record should be kept of each student who attends the school. This record will record attendance records, grade reports and test scores for the student for every year that he/she attends the school. A copy of the record should be made available if the student transfers to another school. The school will also keep personnel files on each staff member. Included in the personnel file should be the job application, resume, transcripts, credential papers, job description (signed by the employee and administrator), annual evaluations, and any other pertinent information. The staff member should be allowed to review all items kept in his/her file. In addition to these major files will be property management and financial records.

At the front desk the secretary should have a check in/out card for each student. The card should have the student's name, parent's names, address, telephone number, and a list of people who are authorized to check the student out in case of illness or an emergency. The student's class schedule and room number should also be on the card. There should be space on the card for the person who checks a student in or out to sign, date, and put the time of check in or check out. These cards should be maintained in a box in alphabetical order by the student's last name. The secretary and administrator also should have a master schedule for the school with rosters for each class.

Safety drills such as fire and tornado drills should be scheduled and a record kept of each drill. Safety is of ultimate importance in a school.

Public Relations/Marketing

Another area of concern is public relations. It is important for the school to present itself in a favorable way to the public. Of course the outside appearance of the buildings and grounds is the first impression people get of the school. So it is important to maintain the buildings and grounds and to keep them clean and free of debris.

The school should also consider having a website to inform people about the school. The website should be easy to use and should be informative. It should have a professional appearance and be free of pop-ups or advertisements. It is a good idea to look at websites for other Christian schools to get ideas for designing a school website. The first page should be simple and easily loaded with tabs to the other pages of the website. Each page should have the tabs included for easy navigation of the website. Include on the first page basic information about the school, i.e. the name of the school and basic contact information. The website should include tabs for a "Statement of Belief's", History of the School, Philosophy of Education, Mission Statement, and Goals. Also include a school calendar. You may want to include a tab on your website where people can make online donations or you can provide information on how a potential donor can make a donation by mail or by phone. You may want to include a page for people wanting to apply for a staff position at your school. It is helpful to provide a page for Frequently Asked Questions. Here you can list typical questions that have been asked about your school with answers. Include a search button on the page for people to search for the questions they have. Other information to include on the website may be the application process, tuition, discounts and scholarships that are available, the day-to-day operation of the school, policies for parent volunteers, dress code/uniforms, Spiritual issues, and academic issues. It is also helpful to have a page for each class. The individual teachers can each design a page and keep it updated.

It is vital that the entire website be kept up-to-date. It is better not to have a website at all if you are not able to keep it fresh with up-to-date information and pictures

Just remember that there are many Christian schools that have websites. Look them up on the Internet to get ideas. When looking at them think of what a parent might want to find on such a website if they are considering enrolling their child in a Christian school, what a parent of enrolled students might want to find, or what a prospective teacher might be looking for, etc. Then plan your website with these points in mind.

Another suggestion is to have a weekly or monthly newsletter. This can be in print form and/or posted on the school's website. It can also be e-mailed to the parents or other interested parties.

There are many other ways to get the word out about your

school. One great way is to host an open house that is open to the public. At the open house have plenty of flyers and business cards available for people interested in learning more about your school.

Be sure to have your school listed on all lists of private schools in your community such as telephone books, newspapers, and information provided for new families that come into the community. Ask local churches if you can place information about your school in their buildings, perhaps a poster on a bulletin board or flyers on the table in the church foyer. Some churches have space in their weekly bulletins or newsletters for community information. Also consider joining the local Chamber of Commerce and other civic organizations. These are just a few ways of getting the word out about your school.

Financial Practices

Accurate financial records are essential. The school must develop a budget and a financial support plan for the annual budget and for long-term requirements. There are many questions to consider. How much funding will be needed and how much will be available? These may be significantly different amounts. Are there methodologies and tools available that will help in these decisions?

A good place to start is to plan the annual budget and project the long-term needs. A key to success is to know as closely as possible the potential financial resources that can be counted on to support the school and then to develop the necessary plans to tap these resources effectively. Most schools probably underestimate the potential financial resources present in the community. Normally, financial support follows mission planning, not the reverse; people respond best to personal appeals that are tied directly to purposes and causes. An effective plan includes financial implications and a design to attain the financial support necessary to implement the plan adequately.

Develop a five-year budget based on the goals of the strategic plan. The financial expert on the board should take responsibility for this. As always you should project assumptions conservatively. Also you should map out the school's accounting procedures: record keeping, check signing, disbursements, petty cash, bank accounts, reconciling bank accounts, and set up an audit committee.

The annual budget is much more than a blueprint for fiscal oversight. It is really a fundamental expression of the school's mission. A quick scan should enable you to determine the school's ability or intent to invest in any number of areas, such as financial aid, faculty compensation and professional development, outreach, facilities upkeep and repair, and the endowment. The budget can be a very clear indication of the school's values, priorities and objectives for the next period.

Given a budget's central role in reflecting a school's values, transparency is crucial. Educating donors, parents, and faculty about the budget process ensures that everyone has an appropriate stake in the financial well being of the school.

Tuition increase letters and open forums, among other examples, provide opportunities for open communication between the school and parents, demonstrating just how their tuition dollars are being spent. Establishing credibility with donors is essential. They must have a clear sense as to exactly how their funds are being used.

Most school budgets list their revenue items from largest to smallest followed by expenditures largest to smallest. On the income side, tuition is typically the largest revenue line item, followed by various types of contributed income, such as the annual fund. Financial aid and tuition remission are listed on the revenue side as a contra-revenue line below tuition—meaning that financial aid diminishes gross tuition, leaving a net tuition figure. Ideally, a school's net tuition—that is, total tuition minus financial aid—should cover as many expenses as possible.

Start with personnel salaries on the expense side. This often comprises of 70 to 80 percent of a school's budget. Include all administrative positions, as well as all support staff, from the janitors to the dietary workers. Don't forget ancillary positions, such as a school nurse or counselor. Add the salaries of every teacher and aid worker. Next, add insurance costs, sick and vacation pay, payroll taxes and other benefits. Though private schools may feel as if they cannot compensate teachers as well as public schools do, it's important to build compensation increases into multi-year strategic financial plans and budgets.

Although they are not budgeted alongside compensation, professional development opportunities attest to a school's investment in its workforce. It has been recommended that 1.5 to 2 percent of a school's budget be earmarked for professional development. Professional development is the key component of maintaining (or improving) a faculty growth culture. This means a faculty made up of teachers who are constantly pushing themselves to improve, which in turn guarantees better student learning.

If your school has any contract labor costs such as ground workers add these costs.

Next, factor in the cost of running the physical facility. Add the yearly utility costs and other normal day-to-day maintenance costs. This could include plumbing and electrical repair, painting, and floor or ceiling repair.

Another important budget item is the cost of supplies. Add up the cost of toilet paper, paper towels, cleaning supplies, light bulbs, pails, buckets, and mops. Include instructional supplies and textbooks. Don't forget paper for copy machines, printer paper and all required forms that are needed to run a school.

Next include the cost of machinery and equipment. Computers need to be replaced occasionally; overhead projectors and other teaching aids must be repaired or replaced yearly. Average in this cost and include it in your yearly budget. Even the school bells and intercom system may need repair or replacement.

Sports equipment must be replaced or repaired. Add in the costs of basketballs, goals, footballs, soccer or any other sports equipment to be used within the school year. Don't forget the cost of any other extracurricular clubs and activities.

The school grounds and parking lots need to be taken care of yearly. Include a line item for outside repairs and upkeep.

It is also crucial for schools to build up surpluses into their annual budgets in order to develop a cash reserve. Schools should build a cash reserve that eventually equals 15 percent of their budget. This will help with sustainability of the school.

As for facility upkeep schools should set aside up to three percent of their plant replacement cost annually for a facility reserve, with 1.5 to 2 percent for renewal projects (i.e. leaking roofs), and 0.5 to 1.5 percent for adaptation (i.e. remodeling). This may be unrealistic for some schools. Therefore, schools should determine their needs through an audit, and then set a percentage that is viable and won't be compromised as other needs arise.

Short-term deficits are acceptable if monies have been earmarked for a strategic or designated purpose, but continual operating deficits erode a school's net worth and, over a few years, can put the life of the school in jeopardy.

A simplified outline for a school budget might look like this.

Revenue and Support
- Tuition and Fees
- Less: Financial Aid and Tuition Remission
- Net Tuition and Fees
- Annual Fund Contributions (event proceeds, contributions, direct donor solicitation)
- Other Income (including program fees, interest and endowment income)

Expenses
- Personnel Costs (includes salary and wages and benefits expenses)
- Instructional Materials and Supplies
- Administration and General Supplies
- Occupancy (Including the Cost of Regular Upkeep of Facilities)
- Development and Fundraising
- Auxiliary Services

Transfers
- Cash reserves for "rainy days"
- Facility renewal, replacement, and special maintenance
- Other strategic priorities

The process of planning a budget is linked with a school's overall mission. Planned expenditures should be developed from the ground up, with each department estimating their needs using a careful approach that justifies how the requested funds achieve the goals of the department and the entire school. The annual budget provides a preeminent opportunity for administrators to evaluate their programs to determine which components have been effective and which have not been effective. When a school builds a budget based on an evaluation of current practice, you get not only a financial projection of needs, but also a comprehensive evaluation of what works and what doesn't work. Furthermore, the annual budget should always be prepared within the context of a strategic multiyear financial plan, which should include a financial model to be monitored and updated annually.

The strategic plan is the beginning of the budget. It predetermines the rate of tuition increases, and it predetermines the total operating budget. Of course, if more resources are needed then the strategic plan makes it easy for the board to make an informed choice about tuition increases to support annual changes.

The following sample budget calendar might be helpful to use when setting up a budget. It is adapted from Business Management for Independent Schools, 5th Edition, published by the National Association of Independent Schools (NAIS). [40]

November: Each department head along with key

administrators are asked to propose preliminary budgets for their areas of responsibility (excluding salary items).

December: Department heads encourage teachers to be creative and forward looking in proposing expenditures that will strengthen their areas within the school. Wish list items can represent goals to work towards over multiple years.

January: Business manager, with the school administrator, reviews departmental budget proposals and produces an overall preliminary balanced budget. The draft should be reviewed with the finance committee of the board of trustees. The overall board should vote on the preliminary budget in mid-winter

February: Business manager reports board approval to department heads and professional staff members. Tuition levels are announced, faculty contracts are drawn, and financial aid guidelines are set.

March to June: Final changes to budget are made based on new information concerning enrollment levels, inflation rates, and educational program decisions. The finance committee approves changes and then the Board of Trustees makes final decisions on the budget, as early as June.

After you have your budget in place it will be time to make plans for any fund raising campaigns. Resist the urge to jump in. Develop a capital campaign and case statement methodically and then implement it systematically. You should develop a Pre-Campaign Capacity Study to determine:

- Available income from tuition
- How much can be raised in your community

- What are the priorities to give to in your community
- Who will give to what causes
- Present gift levels and chart
- System and Approach
- Time Lines
- Campaign Leadership Team
- Gift Categories (e.g. naming of buildings)
- Major donors and how much they can give.

Form a Development Committee to lead this. Experts say that you should raise at least 50% of the funds before you even announce the campaign. Your strategic plan is important at this stage as it provides potential donors concrete evidence of your vision where the donor can fit in, and what your financial priorities are.

These are just a few suggestions about managing finances for a Christian school. Talk to administrators of other schools to get more detailed information and examples. Remember that accurate record keeping is vital. Develop a record keeping system and make it a priority to keep your records current.

Professional Ethics

Christian schools must adhere to professional ethical standards and hold all staff members to a Biblical standard of ethics and conduct themselves in a manner that, according to Ephesians 4:1, is "worthy of the calling [they] have received". [41] The educator should understand that all things should be focused around God, who we are in Christ, our authority and responsibilities to God and others, and our purpose as individuals and as a body. Part of the responsibility of the professional Christian educator is to care for each student's body, soul and spirit. The educator, believing in the worth and dignity of each human being, recognizes the supreme importance of the pursuit of truth, devotion to excellence, and the nurture of the democratic principles. Essential to these goals is the protection of freedom to learn and to teach and the guarantee of equal educational opportunity for all. The educator accepts the responsibility to adhere to the highest ethical standards.

The educator recognizes the magnitude of the responsibility inherent in the teaching process. The desire for the respect and confidence of one's colleagues, of students, of parents, and of the members of the community provides the incentive to attain and maintain the highest possible degree of ethical conduct. The Code of Ethics of the Education Profession indicates the aspiration of all educators and provides standards by which to judge conduct.

The following is an example of principles that may be included in a code of ethical standards for a Christian school.

PRINCIPLE I: Commitment to the Student

The educator strives to help each student realize his or her potential as a worthy and effective member of the body and society. The educator therefore works to stimulate the spirit of inquiry, the acquisition of knowledge, a closer walk with God, wisdom and understanding, and the thoughtful formulation of worthy goals.

In fulfillment of the obligation to the student, the educator–
1.   Shall not unreasonably restrain the student from independent action in the pursuit of learning.
2.   Shall not unreasonably deny the student's access to varying points of view.
3.   Shall not deliberately suppress or distort subject matter

relevant to the student's progress.

4. Shall make reasonable effort to protect the student from conditions harmful to learning or to health and safety.
5. Shall not intentionally expose the student to embarrassment or disparagement.
6. Shall not on the basis of race, color, creed, sex, national origin, marital status, political or religious beliefs, family, social or cultural background, unfairly--
   a. Exclude any student from participation in any program
   b. Deny benefits to any student
   c. Grant any advantage to any student
7. Shall not use professional relationships with students for private advantage.
8. Shall not disclose information about students obtained in the course of professional service unless disclosure serves a compelling professional purpose or is required by law.

PRINCIPLE II: Commitment to the Profession

The education profession is vested by the public with a trust and responsibility requiring the highest ideals of professional service.

The quality of the services of the education profession directly influences the body, nation, citizens, and its outcomes. The educator shall exert every effort to raise professional standards, to promote a climate that encourages the exercise of professional judgment, and to achieve conditions that attract persons worthy of the trust to careers in education.

1. Shall not in an application for a professional position deliberately make a false statement or fail to disclose a material fact related to competency and qualifications.
2. Shall not misrepresent his/her professional qualifications.

3. Shall not assist any entry into the profession of a person known to be unqualified in respect to character, education, or other relevant attribute.
4. Shall not knowingly make a false statement concerning the qualifications of a candidate for a professional position.
5. Shall not disclose information about colleagues obtained in the course of professional service unless disclosure serves a compelling professional purpose or is required by law.
6. Shall not knowingly make a false or malicious statements about a colleague.
7. Shall not accept any gratuity, gift, or favor that might impair or appear to influence professional decisions or action.

The Association of Christian Schools International has a very good article concerning a Code of Ethics for board members posted on their website. [42]

It would be a good idea to check with other Christian School organizations to get help with writing a Code of Ethics for your school.

Remember that we are responsible both to God and to each other and God holds us to the highest standards. Integrity is one of the foundational pillars on which Christian education stands. The more that virtue is exercised, the more entrenched it becomes in one's nature. Integrity implies purity of heart and adherence to sound moral principles in a person's every thought and action. Integrity implies openness, honesty, authenticity, and reliability. Similar to a plumb line that is perfectly perpendicular because of the earth's gravity, integrity permeates a life with genuineness because of its alignment with the principles of God's Word. Conversely, a lying tongue is one of the seven things that are detestable to God. (Proverbs 6:16–19). [43]

End Notes

[1] Proverbs 3:5-6 (All Scripture references are from the NIV translation unless otherwise noted.)

[2] Walter G. Fremont, Teacher to Teacher, October 2003, Bob Jones University Press.

[3] Proverbs 3:5-6

[4] Richard J. Edlin, "Core Beliefs and Values of a Christian Philosophy of Education" in Foundations of Christian School Education, ed. James Braley, Jack Layman, and Ray White, (Purposeful Design Publications, 2003), p. 69.

[5] John 14:6

[6] Kenneth O. Gangel, "Biblical Foundations of Education," in Foundations of Christian School Education, ed. James Braley, Jack Layman, and Ray White, (Purposeful Design Publications, 2003), p. 59.

[7] Ibid. p. 56.

[8] 2 Peter 1:3

[9] Kenneth O. Gangel, "Biblical Foundations of Education," in Foundations of Christian School Education, ed. James Braley, Jack Layman, and Ray White, (Purposeful Design Publications, 2003), p. 60.

[10] Mark 8:36

[11] 1 Timothy 6:10

[12] Genesis 2:24

[13] Richard J. Edlin, "Core Beliefs and Values of a Christian Philosophy of Education" in Foundations of Christian School Education, ed. James Braley, Jack Layman, and Ray White, (Purposeful Design Publications, 2003), p. 79.

[14] Deuteronomy 6:4-9

[15] Douglas Wilson, The Case for Classical Christian Education,

(Wheaton, Illinois: Crossway Books, 2003), 59.

[16] Ibid., 57.

[17] Douglas Wilson, Standing on the Promises (Moscow, Idaho: Cannon Press, 1997), 94.

[18] Psalm 78:1-8

[19] Charles Colson and Nancy Pearcey, How Now Shall We Live, (Wheaton, Illinois: Tyndale House Publishers, 1999), 338.

[20] Lois E. LeBar, Education That Is Christian, (Westwood, New Jersey: Fleming H. Revell Company, 1958), 50.

[21] Ibid.

[22] Harro Van Brummelen, "Understanding Curriculum Design", Foundations of Christian School Education p. 187.

[23] Ibid., 188-190.

[24] Matt 22:37-39 and Romans 12:2, 9-21

[25] 1 Corinthians 2:16

[26] Matt 28:18-20

[27] Ibid., 192-197.

[28] Nancy Ferguson, Christian Educators' Guide to Evaluating and Developing Curriculum, (Valley Forge, PA: Judson Press, 2008).

[29] Ibid., 13-14.

[30] Luke 6:40

[31] James W. Braley, "Training World Christians," in Foundations of Christian School Education, eds. James W. Braley, J. Layman, and R. White (Colorado Springs, Colorado: Purposeful Design Publications, 2003), pp. 322 and 329.

[32] Ferguson p. 100.

[33] Ellen Laurie Black, "The Teacher," in Foundations of Christian School Education, eds. James W. Braley, J. Layman, and R. White (Colorado Springs, Colorado: Purposeful Design Publications, 2003), pp. 147-149.

[34] Proverbs 1:7

[35] Proverbs 23:13

36 Logos School of Casa Grande, AZ, "Handbook for Students and Parents" (2011).

37 Logos School of Casa Grande, AZ, "Student Code of Conduct" (2011).

38 Ephesians 4:1

39 Proverbs 24:3-4

40 Business Management for Independent Schools, 5th Edition, published by the National Association of Independent Schools (NAIS)

41 Ephesians 4:1

42 David Manley, Professional Growth: Establishing a Code of Ethics for the School Board, ACSI, http://www.acsi.org/LinkClick.aspx?fileticket=nbdELLjwXBo%3d&tabid=681.

43 Proverbs 6:16–19.

BIBIOGRAPHY

Anthony, J. Michael, ed. Introducing Christian Education: Foundations for the Twenty-first Century. Grand Rapids, Michigan: Baker Academic, 2001.

Braley, James, J. Layman, and R. White, eds. Foundations of Christian School Education. Colorado Springs, Colorado: Purposeful Design Publications. 2003.

Clark, Robert E., L. Johnson, and A. K. Sloat, eds. Christian Education: Foundations for the Future. Chicago: Moody Press. 1991.

Colson, Charles, and Pearcey, Nancy. How Now Shall We Live. Wheaton, Illinois. Tyndale House Publishers. 1999.

Dockery, David S. and Gregory Alan Thornbury, eds. Shaping A Christian Worldview. Nashville, Tennessee: B & H Publishers. 2002.

Edlin, Richard J. The Cause of Christian Education. Colorado Springs, Colorado: Association of Christian Schools International. 1999.

Estep, James R., Jr., M. J. Anthony, and G. R. Allison, eds. A Theology for Chrisitan Education. Nashville, Tennessee: B & H HPublishing Group. 2008.

Ferguson, Nancy. Christian Educators' Guide to Evaluating and Developing Curriculum. Valley Forge, Pennsilvania: Judson Press. 2008.

Fremont, Walter G. Teacher to Teacher. Bob Jones University Press. October 2003.

Gangel, Kenneth O., and Howard G. Hendricks, eds. The Christian Educator's Handbook on Tching. Grand Rapids, Michigan: Baker Books. 1988.

LeBar, Lois E. Education That Is Christian. Westwood, New Jersey: Fleming H. Revell Company. 1958.

Parrett, Gary A., and S. Steve Kang. Teching the Faith, Forming the Faithful. Downers Grove, Illinois: InterVarsity Press. 2009.

Perks, Stephen C. The Chrisan Philosophy of Education Explained. Whitby, England: Avant Books. 1992.

Powers, Bruce P., ed. Christian Education Handbook, 2nd ed. Nashville, Tennessee: B & H Publishers. 1996.

Richards, Lawrence O. Christian Education: Seeking to Become Like Jesus Christ. Grand Rapids, Michigan: Ministry Resources Library. 1975.

Ringenberg, William C. The Christian College: A History of Protestant Higher Education in America, 2nd ed. GrandRapids, Michigan: Baker Academic. 2006.

Tye, Karen B. Basics of Christian Education. St. Louis, Missouri: Chalice Press. 2000.

Tye, Karen B. Christian Education in the Small Membership

Church. Nashville, Tennessee: Abingdon Press. 2008.

Wells, William V. The Life and Public Services of Samuel Adams. Boston: Little, Brown & Co., 1865.

Wilson, Douglas. The Case for Classical Christian Education. Wheaton, Illinois: Crossway Books. 2003.

Wilson, Douglas. Standing on the Promises. Moscow, Idaho: Cannon Press. 1997.